Principles of Contracting for Project Management

Second Edition

Yanping Chen, PhD, PMP
J. Davidson Frame, PhD, PMP

UMT Press

TABLE OF CONTENTS

THE UMT SERIES ON PROJECT MANAGEMENT PRINCIPLES AND PRACTICES

This book is the second in a series that UMT has put together to provide readers with an overview of the tools, techniques, procedures and issues in selected areas of project management practice. The first was titled *Project Finance: Tools and Techniques*. The third is *Project Office*, authored by Thomas Block and J. Davidson Frame.

We have embarked on this effort in response to growing demand from our students for succinct books that present the tools, techniques and processes used in various project management functional areas in a concise, easy to comprehend and practical format in order to reduce the drudgery of trying to understand and use "boring" and sometimes abstract tools and techniques.

Each book in the series concentrates on one topic of project management practice. It is designed to provide the reader with an understanding of the key tools, techniques and procedures relevant to that practice area. The mechanics and the theories behind the tools, techniques and procedures are explained to facilitate the reader's comprehension and ability to use them. Additionally, practical examples and exercises have been included to give readers hands-on insights.

It is our hope that students who are new to project management will find these books useful. We also hope that project management veterans will be able to use them to refresh their knowledge on current project management practice.

Preface to the 2ND Edition

Procurement and contracting have become popular practices among managers these days because companies have learned to appreciate their potential as sources of efficiency and competitive advantage. Intense global competition has forced companies and organizations to place a high premium on efficiency. This in turn has led to a rethinking of how organizations should run their operations. The trend now is to have companies focus on carrying out their core business activities (what they can do best) and to "cede" the non-strategic aspects of their operations to outsiders in order to tap into the outsiders' strengths. In this way companies expect to reap the benefits of both internal and external competencies.

Such trends have put procurement and contracting management onto the radar screens of corporate managers. However, as with most aspects of life, getting it right requires substantial effort. The business press is filled with stories of contracts that have gone awry. Cost overruns, schedule slippages, poor quality work, acrimonious disputes, and law suits are some of the problems that are associated with the shadow side of contracting. The mere act of contracting does not guarantee desired results.

Some of the factors that have accounted for contracting problems include poor solicitation planning and inefficient contract administration. Another problem is that often personnel are assigned to work on contracts without adequate knowledge and skills in the mechanics and nuances of contracting and procurement. In this case, these people find themselves managing contracts accidentally. Their employers expect them to pick up procurement and contracting skills on the job. Certainly, "learning by doing" has its benefits. But in an environment where subtle nuances make a big difference and mistakes have economic and legal consequences, this approach has clear limitations.

The fact is that contract management requires some measure of formal training, specialization and possibly certification. But the learning does not end with formal training or certification. There is an abundance of perspectives, issues, tools and techniques that the student of procurement and contracting needs to master.

This book strives to present readers with practical insights into the theory and practice of contracting in project environments. It is *not* a book on contract law. Rather, its focus is on the business and behavioral aspects of contracting on projects. It views contracting as a vehicle to enable business and government enterprises to achieve their business goals. It recognizes that people lie at the heart of contracting efforts. Consequently, effective contracting requires the players to take into account their different values and negotiating strengths. It requires them to recognize that the best contracts reflect win-win solutions, where all parties to the contract feel that it serves their interests to follow its terms and conditions.

This second edition of *Principles of Contracting for Project Management* is geared to providing the novice with key insights needed to understand the rationale and process of contracting in project environments. Information contained in the first edition has been updated, but not radically altered. The biggest difference between this new edition and the first edition has been the addition of Chapter 9, which presents a brief overview of performance-based contracting. Over the past few years, perspectives on how major systems should be procured and managed have undergone dramatic change. The performance-based contracting perspective holds that effective contracting of complex systems requires buyers to specify *what* they need. This is done by defining clearly the performance outcomes they seek. The contractor's job is to determine *how* the performance outcomes can be achieved. This perspective differs substantially from the traditional approach, where buyers often defined their needs by telling contractors *how* to do their jobs.

CONTENTS OF BOOK

This book steps through the entire procurement life cycle, from procurement planning through contract close-out.. Following is a brief description of the contents of each chapter.

Chapter 1: Introduction shows how contracting out work is a growing phenomenon that reflects today's business exigencies. It describes the procurement life cycle and identifies strengths and weaknesses inherent in contracting.

Chapter 2: Procurement Planning provides insights into the issues and activities that need to be addressed in the earliest stages of preparing to formulate a contract. It identifies key elements of the statement of work (SOW). It also investigates how the contract effort should be structured – either as a cost reimbursable effort, or firm fixed price effort.

Chapter 3: Solicitation Planning examines the steps that need to be carried out in order to prepare to solicit bidders on a contract. It highlights the difference between negotiated (using RFPs) and non-negotiated (using IFBs) bids, and competitive and non-competitive bids (e.g., on sole source solicitations). It also shows how bids are typically structured.

Chapter 4: Preparing the Bid illustrates the steps contractors take in order to bid on an award, beginning with making bid/no-bid decisions through the writing of proposals.

Chapter 5: Source Selection/Contract Award describes how buyers review and prioritize bids to determine which contractor wins the award. It also discusses how typical contracts are negotiated and, ultimately, formulated.

Chapter 6: Post Contract Award/Contract Administration looks at life *after* the contract award is made. It examines the roles of different players on both the buyer and contractor side during the period the contract effort is carried out.

Chapter 7: Contract Close Out describes the steps that need to be taken to bring a contract to an orderly conclusion. It also looks at situations where contracts are terminated before they have run their full course.

Chapter 8: Odds and Ends reviews a number of different types of contracts that business managers come across during the course of their regular business activities, including employee contracts, non-disclosure agreements, non-competition agreements, intellectual property agreements, and licensing agreements.

Chapter 9.Performance Based Contracting provides a quick overview of what is becoming the dominant approach to handling contracts for the development of major systems. It is based on the view that buyers should define their requirements in terms of measurable performance outcomes. The contractor's job is to figure out *how* the work effort should be carried out, so that the measurable performance outcomes are achieved.

Chapter 10: Conclusion revisits the argument that contracts play a central role in organizations today. It promotes the view that effective contracting requires that key players have solid knowledge and skills in the contract management arena.

CHAPTER ONE
INTRODUCTION

OVERVIEW

One of the discernible characteristics distinguishing today's organizations from past ones is the new emphasis on contracting out work. Project professionals now find themselves routinely working with contract workers on a daily basis or working as members of contractor project teams. This should not be surprising. Contracting out work is a natural consequence of organizational evolution and a response to environmental dynamics. Competitive pressures are forcing organizations to rethink how they spend their money. Not long ago, the power and prestige of a company was linked to its size. Companies with huge payrolls that produced a wide variety of goods were the most highly admired. Today, however, big is not better. Beginning in the late 1980s and early 1990s, business and government organizations undertook major steps toward downsizing in order to become "lean" and "nimble." In producing goods and services, they began to differentiate between those that enhanced their core competencies, and those that were marginal. This move toward downsizing and streamlining was part of what was called the *business process reengineering* movement.

In this new environment, organizations found themselves continually faced with make-or-buy decisions. That is, an organization must determine whether to *make* the product or service internally (using internal resources) or *buy* it from outside sources. It must be noted that the make-or-buy decision is not strictly an either/or decision. It presents managers with a range of options from which they can make a choice depending on the level of customization required, resource requirements, and the degree of difficulty and risk. For example, when a company considers deploying new proprietary software, it has three options: either to develop the proprietary software in-house using its own resources; or to use external resources to carry out the project; or to use a combination of internal and external resources.

The process of acquiring and using outside resources either fully or partially is known as *outsourcing*. The process involves contracting in one form or another. When organizations use outsourcing to procure external resources they are described as *buyers*. Those who provide goods and services to buyers under contract are called *contractors*.

Rising Incidence of Outsourcing

Outsourcing is not a new phenomenon. It has been practiced extensively on large capital projects in the military and the construction industries for many years. The great bulk of weapons systems procured by the US military has relied on the work of contractors since before the Civil War in the mid-19th century. Initially, contracting focused on the purchase of weapons and supplies, where the military would provide specifications that needed to be met and contractors would build to the specs. Beginning with World War II, the acquisition system had evolved to the point where the military explicitly funded *projects* that addressed the development of sophisticated deliverables. The Manhattan Project to build an atomic bomb was the most famous of these projects.

The construction industry has depended on outsourcing different pieces of construction projects for decades. A prime contractor is selected through a competitive bid process. The prime contractor, in turn, selects sub-contractors who perform specialized work, e.g., pouring the foundation, installing windows, wiring the building, installing the plumbing. On large construction projects, a substantial portion of the project superintendent's job is managing subcontractors.

In recent years, all industries have increased their employment of outsourcing. Major companies like IBM, which until recently was largely autarchic, began divesting themselves of non-essential project and production activities in the 1990s in order to focus on carrying out their core business. While US enterprises led the outsourcing movement, it was clear by the early 2000s that Europeans were heavily engaged in outsourcing efforts as well. Interestingly, a growing portion of outsourced efforts were being carried out in developing countries on behalf of industrial leaders.

This was most evident in the outsourcing of software services to Indian programmers by Western enterprises.

REASONS FOR OUTSOURCING GOODS AND SERVICE

Organizations outsource goods and service for a number of reasons. For example:

- *To reduce and control costs*
  Outsourcing can lead to cost savings in many ways. For example, with outsourcing, you pay for work services only when you need them – when the work stops, so do the payments. Another example: With outsourcing, you can lessen costly fringe benefit expenses.

- *To gain access to world-class expertise and specialized skills*
  No organization possesses all the insights and skills it needs. It must turn to the outside world to gain access to them.

- *To gain access to new technology*
  Technology is distributed among organizations throughout the world. It is often protected by patents, which limit access to it among non-patent holders. Often, the only access to the technology is through licensing arrangements – licenses are a form of contract.

- *To improve the company's focus*
  Companies have come a long way since Ford experimented with its self-contained River Rouge manufacturing plant in the early twentieth century. Senior managers recognize that it does not make economic sense to try to do everything. Beyond this, they see that by trying to be entirely self-sufficient, they lose focus as to their principal business purpose. With outsourcing, they can focus on developing their core capabilities in-house while conducting peripheral activities by using outsiders.

- *To free resources for other purposes*
  It often happens that an organization's best workers are in such great demand that they are stretched thin. In this situation, it may make sense to hire outsiders temporarily to take care of routine chores, thereby freeing the most valuable resources to do what they do best.

- *To deal with functions that are difficult to manage*
  A small company may find that it lacks the skills and desire to carry out the payroll function, so it may outsource this function to a contractor. Similarly, many companies outsource the public relations function because they recognize that an outside expert can do a better job, more cheaply, than an internal public relations department.

- *To share risks*
  A key component of partnering arrangements that are so popular today is risk sharing. These partnering arrangements are governed by contracts, which define who has what roles and responsibilities. The assignment of roles and responsibilities has the effect of apportioning risk to the different partners. If X happens, then Partner A assumes the risk, while if Y happens, risk is carried by Partner B.

- *To improve cash flow*
  This point can be best explained by means of an example: Fabulous Toys, Inc., finds that it can build a manufacturing facility in Iowa to produce its plastic toys, or it can outsource the manufacturing effort to plants in Shenzhen, China. The build-in-Iowa option would entail a major investment that would tie up cash flow for years. However, the outsource-in-China option would enable Fabulous Toys to pursue a pay-as-you-go strategy, avoiding the tying up of capital in an expensive investment.

THE DOWNSIDE OF OUTSOURCING

Contracting has its share of well-known problems. Examples include inadequate performance by the contractor, sudden declaration of bankruptcy by the contractor, conflicting interests of buyer and contractor, and a buyer's refusal to pay for unauthorized work done by the contractor. The common problems can lead to acrimonious conflicts, some of which end up in the courts. We shall discuss the resolution of disputes in some detail later (see Chapter 6).

Beyond these problems, there is the broader issue of the "hollowing" of technical capabilities that outsourcing can create. This problem was evident in the 1980s, when President Ronald Reagan's Office of Federal Procurement Policy did all that it could to get government agencies to outsource many of their activities to private sector contractors. Engineering and computer services were easy targets for outsourcing. Consequently, in their rush to downsize and outsource, many Federal agencies lost their ability to carry out technical work. In fact, their technical capabilities were so diminished that they were not even able to assess the technical merits of contractor proposals! Consequently, the excessive dependence on outside contractors led to a lessening of government effectiveness in some areas.

In view of the pervasive use of contracting in both public and private organizations, it is important for project managers and team members to have a broad understanding of the key issues and mechanics of contracting. It is also important for them to acquire skills that will enable them to better manage the procurement and contracting process in their organizations.

PROCUREMENT MANAGEMENT PROCESS

In its *A Guide to the Project Management Body of Knowledge* (3rd ed., 2005), the Project Management Institute (PMI) has identified *procurement management* as one of the nine knowledge areas that constitute the core knowledge of project management. According to PMI, the procurement management process includes the following:

- Procurement planning: determining what to procure and when
- Solicitation planning: documenting product requirements and identifying potential sources
- Solicitation: obtaining quotations, bids, offers or proposals
- Source selection: choosing from among potential sources
- Contract administration: managing the contractual relationship with the contractor
- Contract closeout: completion and settlement of the contract, including resolution of any open items.

We shall follow PMI's characterization of the procurement management process throughout this book. Each of these six elements of the procurement management process will be covered in a separate chapter.

Two Important Principles

Before delving into the details of the contract and procurement life-cycle, we believe it is wise to raise two abiding principles. It is easy to lose sight of them once you begin reviewing contracting vocabulary, concepts, techniques and experiences, so we place them at the outset of the book to emphasize their importance. The principles are:

- On contracts, everything is negotiable
- Parties to a contract should strive for win-win solutions

Each of these important principles will be discussed briefly.

On Contracts, Everything Is Negotiable

Novices to contracting often approach contracts too narrowly. In their jobs, they may have worked with a contract template that is structured in such-and-such a way and contains this-and-that provisions. This template becomes their model for contracting and they never dare deviate from it. Whenever they enter into new contractual arrangements, they make some minor adjustments to the template document and that's that.

What novices lose sight of is that contracts are formal agreements between two or more parties, and as such they can reflect the needs and demands of the parties in myriad ways. Everything is negotiable on a contract, provided the provisions are legal. For example, if the new CEO of a company successfully negotiates to have the company pay for her opera tickets, then she can have this provision included in her employment contract. Or if a small business owner requires that a contractor employ his incompetent nephew as project manager of a project funded by the owner, then this can be written into the contract. This reality has important implications on how contract documents are physically formulated. You can choose to write a contract that is one sentence long or 1,000 pages long. You can formulate contracts whose terms are written in three languages. You can even write legally binding contracts on paper towels, if that is acceptable to the signatories. The point is that in general, there is no prescribed best way to formulate a contract.

Clearly, there are often practical constraints you face that will affect the best way to formulate your contract. For example, if you wish to enter into a contract with a government agency, you will have to work with their templates. Furthermore, where government is hampered with rules and regulations, you will find that the expression "everything is negotiable" is not entirely true. Another example: By writing a one sentence contract, you may find that it has small value because it describes so little. On the other hand, you may find that writing a 1,000 page contract – where all possible contingencies are covered – leads to a situation where no work can get done owing to the excessive restrictions contained in the contract document.

Ultimately, in formulating a contract and identifying provisions that it should cover, you need to employ a rule of reason. The objective of the document is not to reduce risk to zero. Rather, it is to provide the basis for two or more parties to work together to achieve mutually desired goals.

This brings us to the second principle.

PARTIES TO A CONTRACT SHOULD STRIVE FOR WIN-WIN SOLUTIONS

The best negotiators are people who create win-win situations. They recognize that if you are going to gain commitment from all parties to the negotiated solution, then all parties should believe they have gained something through the negotiation process. If one party feels aggrieved by the outcome, you should not expect it to strive to support the spirit or the letter of the negotiated solution. Consider how many historians believe that World War II had its roots in the Treaty of Versailles, where after World War I the allies unilaterally imposed severe sanctions on Germany. Germany's unhappiness with the provisions of the treaty led to political instability and made Hitler's ascendancy possible.

One-sided contracts lead to trouble. It is tempting for a powerful party to write terms into a contract to the disadvantage of the other, weaker party. While the chief negotiator of this contract might brag about his or her

11

negotiating prowess, this contract has been built on a weak foundation. The weaker party may resent the situation it is in and strive to undermine the agreement. Or conditions may be so unfavorable to the weaker party that it goes out of business!

The best contracts are those where all the signatories are excited about the document and what it represents. The parties see the contract as a vehicle to allow them to achieve their desired goals. They are motivated to move forward to a successful conclusion of the contract.

CHAPTER TWO
PROCUREMENT PLANNING

With procurement planning, managers identify what goods and services they wish to acquire. They then devise an approach to acquiring them. Specifically, during the procurement planning effort, they develop a procurement management plan, a statement of work (SOW), and determine what type of contract should be implemented.

MAKE-OR-BUY ANALYSIS

One of the key activities procurement or contracting managers carry out is to plan for the acquisition of goods and services by means of a contract. In other words, procurement and contracting do not just happen. They require formal planning.

Procurement planning allows managers to decide what to procure and when. In addressing such a decision, one of the first steps they carry out is to conduct make-or-buy analyses. This approach helps them to decide which goods and services should be produced cost-effectively in-house and which should be procured from vendors. In performing a make-or-buy analysis, an appraisal of the costs and benefits of "make" or "buy" options are carefully assessed and the results compared before a final decision is made.

The make or buy decision requires both rigorous financial analysis and subjective expert judgment. For example, a new computer company must decide what portion of the components of its computers it should manufacture and what portion it should buy from suppliers. After conducting a rigorous financial analysis (including a review of investment requirements, tax implications, cash flow position), Michael Dell of Dell Computers used his expert judgment to decide to outsource the production of nearly all the components of his machines. Dell Computers' operations focused on assembling the components and marketing the computers. In the early 2000s, Dell was the most profitable computer company in America.

THE PROCUREMENT MANAGEMENT PLAN

Procurement management plans must be tailored to the circumstances facing the organization and reflect the exigencies of the specific project being pursued. For example, if the organization has a procurement department, then this department will play a lead role in the procurement effort. If it does not, then the customer desiring to acquire goods or services may work with procurement experts, project team members, and others to devise an acquisition strategy.

The procurement management plan itself must address a range of issues, such as:

- Who will play the lead role in the acquisition process?
- What type of contract mode should be employed?
- What should be the timing of the acquisition effort?
- How should the efforts of multiple vendors be coordinated if multiple vendors are employed?
- What pertinent rules and regulations both within the organization and outside need to be addressed during the acquisition effort?

STATEMENT OF WORK (SOW)

In procurement management, a clear description of the goods and services to be provided from outside suppliers is essential. A statement of work (SOW) provides this kind of information. For this reason, a SOW must be detailed enough to enable prospective contractors to understand the requirements and needs of the buyer. According to NASA, well-crafted SOWs play the following roles in the procurement management process:

- *They allow contractors to price their proposal more accurately and submit higher quality technical proposals*
  Vaguely phrased SOWs are subject to multiple interpretations. One potential bidder may interpret the work effort as something substantial, while another may see it to be

something humble. Ultimately, the interpretation given to the vague SOW will affect the accuracy of the cost estimates made regarding the work that needs to be carried out, and will also determine the degree to which the proposed effort hits the target technically.

- *They provide a baseline for the development of other parts of the solicitation, particularly the evaluation criteria, technical proposal instructions and independent cost estimate* Ultimately, the evaluation criteria, technical proposal instructions, and independent cost estimates developed in association with a solicitation are based on the work effort that needs to be carried out, as defined by the SOW. If the SOW is poorly formulated, then other parts of the solicitation will be weak as well.

- *They minimize the need for change orders which can increase cost and delay completion* As mentioned above, vaguely articulated SOWs can be interpreted in different ways. What often happens is that the contractor interprets elements of the SOW in a way that is different from what the buyer intended. Consequently, as the deliverable is being developed and the buyer sees that it is not addressing the intended needs, the buyer is likely to request a change order. The change will drive up project costs and can lead to schedule slippages.

16

- *They allow both the contractor and buyer to assess performance*
  As projects are carried out, standard practice requires progress to be assessed against work and deliverables defined in the SOW. If the SOW is poorly formulated, then this assessment effort becomes difficult to carry out meaningfully.

- *They reduce claims and disputes under a contract*
  A major source of claims (e.g., demands for additional payment to contractors) and disputes is disagreement about the terms and conditions of a contract. If buyer and contractor disagree on what the SOW says, this will likely lead to conflict between the two parties.

Methods of Formulating Statements of Work

A big debate in the contracting arena addresses the general orientation of SOWs and the level of detail they should contain. Basically, there are two schools of thought. One argues that the SOW should be quite detailed, leaving little room for interpretation on the part of the contractor. The point is that if you specify your requirements in detail, you have a good chance of receiving what you requested.

An opposing school of thought holds that the best SOWs are those that sketch out what needs to be done without getting involved with the details. By taking this approach, the buyer enables the contractor to figure out the best solution to addressing the specified needs. Thus the buyer does not presume to have the answers and is signaling the contractor to offer creative solutions.

As often occurs in this type of situation, both arguments have merit – and both have weaknesses. In practice, the approach you take will be governed by the circumstances you face. For example, on routine acquisitions of goods and services – acquisitions you have carried out over years whose details are well known to you – it often makes sense to specify your requirements in detail in the SOW. In this case, you really do know what you want and what it takes to achieve your requirements.

On the other hand, if you are contracting to acquire goods and services in a dynamic area, where technology and the business environment are continually changing, it may make better sense to define what it is that the deliverable should be able to do, and to leave it up to the contractor to determine how the desired functionality can be achieved. By specifying your requirements in detail, you are presuming that you have all the answers – an unlikely eventuality. Furthermore, you are forestalling the possibility that the contractor can come up with an innovative solution. In its extreme form, this second approach to SOW development is captured in a Statement of Objectives – a SOO.

The most experienced buyers in the world are the men and women who work in the US Federal government and acquire goods and services by means of contracts. Within the US Federal acquisition process, SOWs are typically formulated in one of three ways:

- Design/detailed specification SOW
- Level of effort SOW
- Performance based SOW

Each of these approaches will be described briefly.

DESIGN/DETAILED SPECIFICATION SOW

As its name implies, this method produces a detailed SOW that tells the contractor how to do the work. The contractor is required to follow the contents of the SOW exactly. One negative aspect of this approach is that buyers must accept responsibility for any flaws that appear in the SOW and that are passed on to the deliverable. Furthermore, this approach encourages contractors to "manage to the spec" – they will provide buyers what they ask for, even if they identify a better way to deliver a superior product.

LEVEL OF EFFORT SOW

SOWs under this category are usually very broad. They describe the general nature, scope or complexity of the service or products to be provided over a given period of time. They are normally associated with task order and delivery order contracts.

PERFORMANCE-BASED SOW

A performance-based SOW structures all aspects of the procurement around the purpose of the work to be performed. Unlike the design/detailed specification SOW, SOWs of this type do not attempt to dictate how the work is to be performed. They are deliberately written to allow the contractor the freedom to determine how best to accomplish the work. As such, these SOWs maximize the contractors' control over their work and allow for innovation. Performance-based SOWs emphasize performance that can be contractually defined in a manner that allows the contractor's outputs to be measured in terms of technical, quality, schedule, and cost performance. Within the US Federal government, this has become the preferred way of acquiring contracted services.

STATEMENT OF OBJECTIVES (SOO)

As mentioned above, *Statements of Objectives (SOOs)* can be used in lieu of SOWs. A SOO states what the buyer expects from the solicitation. The contractor is expected to formulate a SOW to achieve the buyer's objectives.

STRUCTURING THE CONTRACT

As part of the solicitation planning process, the buyer must determine in advance the structure of the proposed contract. Different types of contracts provide different advantages and risks to buyers and contractors. The types of contracts commonly used in procurement management are: cost plus contracts, firm fixed price contracts, unit based contracts, performance-based contracts. These contract types share risks differently between the buyer and the contractor.

KEY COST VARIABLES IN A CONTRACT

To understand the implications associated with different types of contracts, it is useful to know the meaning of a few important cost concepts. The key cost variables that may be specified in a contract are:

- *Target cost*
  This is the expected cost, negotiated between the buyer and the contractor.

- *Actual cost*
  This is the actual cost incurred for doing the work.

- *Fee*

The amount paid to the contractor, in addition to reimbursable costs. It represents the contractor's profit.

- *Price*
  The amount the buyer pays the contractor for services rendered. It includes reimbursable costs incurred by the contractor, plus the contractor's profit or fee.

- *Cost sharing ratio*
  Applicable when costs are to be shared by the buyer and contractor. It is the percentage of the cost each agrees to share.

COST PLUS (OR COST REIMBURSABLE) CONTRACTS

Under this type of contract, the contractor is reimbursed for all allowable costs associated with the contract effort. The term *allowable cost* is important to understand. The contract must clearly spell out what expenses the contractor can incur. For example, the contractor can incur expenses for the purchase of materials employed to develop the deliverable and to pay for pertinent labor services. These are termed *allowable* costs and will be reimbursed by the buyer. However, costs that have nothing to do with meeting the requirements of the contract will *not* be reimbursed. For example, the buyer will not reimburse the cost of boarding the contractor CEO's pet dog – a notorious incident that actually occurred on a Federal government contract.

Cost reimbursable contracts usually include:

- *An estimate of the project cost*
  A figure that estimates how much the contractor anticipates spending in order to carry out the work defined in the SOW.

- *Provision for reimbursing the contractor's expenses*
  A statement of the process the contractor should carry out to get reimbursed for expenses that are incurred while engaged in contract work. It will cover when reimbursement requests can be made (e.g., monthly), the steps that should be taken when submitting reimbursement requests (e.g., "Reimbursement requests should be made using Form ABC, and should be submitted to the accounts payable office."), and a statement indicating the documentation that must accompany reimbursement requests (e.g., receipts for articles purchased).

- *Provision for paying a fee as the contractor's profit*
  A fee can be paid to the contractor on a *pro rata* basis each month, at the end of the contract, or using a combination of these two approaches, where part of the fee is paid each month, and

part is held back, to be paid as part of the final payment when the contract work is done.

- *A limitation on the buyer's cost liability*
  A ceiling on the total level of expenses the contractor can incur during the life of the contract. A feature of cost plus contracts is that once the allotted funds have been spent, the work stops, even if the contracted deliverables have not been completely delivered. If the buyer wants to continue with the effort, buyer and contractor can negotiate an amendment to the contract, adding extra funds to complete the work. On cost plus fixed fee contracts, buyer and contractor must decide whether an additional fee should be offered for the additional effort.

APPROPRIATENESS OF COST REIMBURSABLE CONTRACTS

In general, cost reimbursable contracts are most appropriate in situations where the work to be performed is not well defined. This is characteristic of first-of-a-kind efforts and risky ventures, where there is little or no performance track record. In such circumstances, high quality contractors are unwilling to work in a fixed price mode, because cost overruns – which are readily possible with ill-defined work – will be paid by them. Consider that a major cost overrun could even put them out of business.

Consequently, most risk on a cost plus contract is borne by the buyer, who agrees to reimburse the contractor for whatever allowable expenses are incurred. Why would a buyer be willing to bear the risk? The answer is simple: High quality contractors do not bid on risky contracts that can put them out of business! Certainly, there are contractors willing to bid on anything, and the danger is that the only bids the buyer receives on solicitations for high risk, fixed price contracts come from low performers.

In this book, we examine four types of cost reimbursable contracts:

- Cost plus fixed fee
- Cost plus incentive fee
- Cost plus award fee
- Time and materials

COST PLUS FIXED FEE (CPFF) CONTRACTS

This type of contract has two components: costs and a fixed fee. Costs include both direct costs (what the contractor spends to carry out the work effort, including direct labor and material costs) and indirect costs (expenses incurred to support the direct work effort, e.g., overhead and fringe benefits). The buyer agrees to reimburse the contractor for allowable costs incurred. Beyond this, the buyer agrees to pay the contractor a fixed fee – i.e., a profit figure negotiated before the work begins – for the contracted work effort.

The reason for offering a *fixed* fee is to remove incentive for the contractor to experience cost overruns. If the fee were tied to expenses incurred, then the contractor would have a strong incentive to spend as much as possible – the more that is spent, the higher the level of profit! However, with a fixed fee, the contractor faces no incentive to spend excessively – regardless of expense levels, the fee is fixed. Fees are determined before contract work begins through a process of negotiation between buyer and contractor.

There are different approaches that can be taken to paying the fee. One is to pay the fee in a *pro rata* fashion. For example, on a four month project, one-fourth of the fee can be paid during each payment period. Another is to pay a fee according to the work that has been performed, e.g., if twenty percent of the work has been achieved, the twenty percent of the fee can be paid. A third approach is to withhold paying any fee until the work has been successfully completed. And finally, a mixed approach may be pursued, where some of the fee is paid throughout the life of the project, and a portion is held back until work has been completed successfully.

The sum of the cost estimate plus fixed fee is the *contract price*.

Example

Infrared, Inc. has contracted Project Search Co. to provide design services for a new software product. The estimated (target) cost of the design effort is $90,000.The two contracting parties agree that the buyer will pay the contractor a fixed fee of $7,000 for providing its services. It is also agreed that the buyer will reimburse the contractor for all allowable costs incurred in doing the work. Thus, the target contract price is $97,000. During the course of carrying out the work effort, the contractor presents the buyer with invoices for $85,000 in services. This reflects total expenses incurred that need to be reimbursed. What is the final contract price?

Final Contract Price = Fixed Fee + Costs
= $7,000   + $85,000 = $92,000

Note that the contractor got the job done for $5,000 cheaper than estimated, yet is still entitled to a $7,000 fee. This is smart policy – you don't want to punish contractors for saving money by reducing their fee.

COST PLUS INCENTIVE FEE (CPIF) CONTRACTS

As with the CPFF mode, CPIF contracts reimburse contractors for their expenses. The big difference is that there is an added incentive to save money or perform ahead of schedule. The incentive is explicitly stated in the form of a payment schedule that defines the size of a bonus paid for different schedule or budget performance scenarios. For example, the statement might stipulate that if the contractor delivers the deliverable a month early, it will receive a $5,000 bonus, or if it delivers a month late, it will have $3,000 deducted from the fee. Bonuses for cost savings are often stated in terms of a sharing ratio that allows buyer and contractor to split the cost savings in a prescribed fashion.

The trick here is to define the target costs accurately. If they are set unrealistically high, this will lead to an undeserved windfall for the contractor. If they are set too low, this may demoralize the contractor, who now faces a situation where it will be penalized for poor performance when such poor performance does not actually exist.

While we have only discussed incentives for cost and schedule performance, incentives for quality performance can be established as well when appropriate. For example, the SOW may specify that a particular software system must be capable of handling 1,000 complex transactions per minute. An incentive system might be established where a $5,000 bonus is paid if the software can handle more than 1,500 complex transactions in a minute.

In theory, the clear stipulation of bonuses/penalties for different levels of performance is a virtue, since it reduces ambiguity. In practice, however, buyers complain that the mechanical application of incentive formulations can work to their disadvantage, because you can have contractors meeting bonus targets even though they have not done particularly good jobs as contractors. For example, a contractor who does not return buyer phone calls, who has not followed required procedures, and who has behaved hostilely toward the buyer's employees is still entitled to a bonus if it delivers under budget or ahead of schedule. To deal with this type of possibility, some buyers prefer to employ a cost plus award fee (CPAF) mechanism. (CPAF modalities will be discussed in the next section.)

EXAMPLE

The contract between Infrared, Inc. and Project Search has been changed into a cost plus incentive fee contract. The following information has been extracted from the contract document.

Target Cost: $90,000
Fixed fee: $7,000
Target Price: $97,000
Sharing ratio: 60:40

The sharing ratio tells us that if actual cost is less than the target cost, buyer will reimburse the contractor the actual cost plus 40% of the amount below the target cost. If actual cost is higher than the target cost, buyer will reimburse the actual cost minus the 40% of the amount above the target cost.

At the end of the project, the contractor reports that its actual cost was $80,000. What is the contract price?

Contract Price = (Target Cost – Actual Cost) x 40% + Actual cost + Fixed Fee
                = ($90,000 - $80,000) x 40% +
                   $80,000 + $7,000
                = $4,000 + $80,000 + $7,000

= $91,000

In calculating profit:

Contractor's Profit = $91,000 - $80,000 = $11,000

In this case, since the actual cost incurred by the contractor is below the target cost by $10,000, the contractor gets a bonus of $4,000 and the buyer makes a cost savings of $6,000 on the contract price – a happy, win-win situation.

EXAMPLE

Target Cost: $90,000
Fixed Fee: $7,000
Actual cost: $89,000
Actual delivery: 10 weeks
Incentive schedule:
- 8 week delivery: $4,000 bonus
- 9 week delivery: no bonus
- 10 week delivery: $2,000 penalty
- Sharing ratio: 50:50

In this case, the contractor gets paid $89,000 (actual cost) plus a fee of $7,000, plus an incentive bonus of $500 (for the cost savings), minus a penalty of $2,000. The final contract price, then, is $94,500.

Cost Plus Award Fee (CPAF) Contracts

As with CPIF contracts, the cost plus award fee (CPAF) contract mechanism attempts to provide incentives for contractors to do their jobs faster, better, and cheaper than stipulated in the contract. The difference between the CPIF and CPAF approaches is that the former offers bonuses/penalties according to objective criteria, whereas the latter depends heavily upon subjective judgment of performance. That is, with CPAF contracts, buyers can award bonuses/penalties according to subjective factors (e.g., attitude of contractor) as well as objective criteria.

To establish an effective CPAF mechanism, a number of steps must be taken. First, the size of an award fee bonus pool must be determined. For example, it may be determined that 10% of the target price can be set aside as money that goes into an award fee pool.

Second, criteria must be established identifying what conditions must be met to lead to the granting of awards. The same type of performance schedules and formulas employed in CPIF contracts can be used, but in this case they serve as guidelines rather than as the sole basis for granting an award. Subjective criteria can also be articulated.

Third, a schedule defining when award reviews will be conducted should be established. For example, on a one year project, it may be stipulated that award reviews will be conducted quarterly.

Fourth, the size of the award pool for each award fee review needs to be determined. A common way of doing this is to make the size of the award proportional to the percentage of work scheduled to be carried out in the review period. Thus if it is estimated that 35% of a contract effort will be executed during a given award review period, then 35% of the award pool should be eligible for being granted during the review.

Finally, as with the other cost reimbursable mechanisms, a fixed fee should be determined before the contract is implemented.

Buyers like CPAF contracts because they give them more leverage over their contractors than CPIF contracts. Contractors, understandably, may be nervous that this process will make buyers excessively demanding. In practice, this last concern does not appear to be a serious problem. In fact, some buyers complain that their award fee panels are too generous in their treatment of contractors – that they wind up awarding most of the award pool to contractors automatically, whether they deserve the bonus or not!

TIME AND MATERIALS CONTRACTS

A time and materials contract reimburses the contractor for labor costs and materials used in doing the contract work. Time and material contracts provide for the payment of direct labor hours at an hourly rate that includes direct labor cost, indirect costs, and profit. The contractor performs the work, documenting the types and quantities of labor used and the cost for parts and materials. Each month, the contractor sends its bills to the buyer for payment based on the agreed upon hourly rates.

Time and material contracts are typically used for repair, maintenance and operations, as well as for consulting and other types of services.

With time and materials contracts, both the buyer and contractor share risk. The contractor may be asked to price its labor without any guaranteed usage level (it may turn out that its services are never used), while the buyer may be uncertain about the number of hours needed to do a job and costs associated with materials.

EXAMPLE

Number of hours required for the work: 200
Hourly rate: $300 (note: includes overhead, fringe benefits and profit)
Cost of materials: $15,000
Contract Price: $60,000 + $15,000 = $75,000

FIRM FIXED PRICE (OR LUMP-SUM) CONTRACTS

Under firm fixed price or "lump sum" contracts, buyers and contractors agree in advance on a price for a defined work effort. Once the price has been agreed upon, the contractor must perform for this price. If the actual cost of the work is greater than the agreed upon price, then the contractor faces a loss. If it is less than the agreed upon price, then the contractor experiences a profit.

Buyers generally like fixed price contracts because the bulk of risk is assumed by the contractor. With cost reimbursable contracts, even the most conscientious contractors do not risk losing their own money when cost overruns occur, so the incentive to save money is not as powerful as when one's own nickel is at risk.

Interestingly, contractors can also favor fixed priced contracts under certain circumstances, because effective, low-cost producers can make substantial profits on such contracts. Consider the contractor who wins a competitive bid to produce 100,000 widgets at $10 each. Let's say that through innovative techniques, solid production processes, and effective management this company can produce each widget at a cost of $4.00. Thus it can realize a gross profit of $6.00 per widget. That works out to a profit of $600,000 on a $1,000,000 contract!

Fixed price contracts are most appropriate when dealing with routine procurements. For example, a company that desires to purchase 10,000 pencils will do so with fixed price contracts. In the project environment, they are appropriate when dealing with projects whose scope is well defined and where the performing organization is experienced in carrying out the defined work. They can be used for large projects as well, so long as these projects entail doing well-defined work. They are least appropriate for speculative projects whose processes and outcomes are poorly defined, for example, state of the art research and development projects.

EXAMPLE

Cost Estimate = $90,000
Estimated profit = $10,000
Contract Price = $100,000

Regardless of the actual cost to the contractor at the completion of the project, the price to the buyer remains $100,000.

ADVANTAGES OF FIRM FIXED CONTRACTS

The principal advantages of firm fixed price contracts go to buyers worried about cost overruns. As already mentioned, an important advantage is that with firm fixed price contracts, buyers limit their risk of cost overruns. If an overrun occurs, the contractor suffers the consequences. Another advantage is that buyers know in advance what contracted goods and services will cost them. They may even be willing to pay a premium for this knowledge. With cost reimbursable contracts, they are never certain what the contract price will ultimately be. Experience shows that serious cost overruns are a continual possibility. Finally, if the firm fixed price contract is well executed and the performer is a high quality, ethical player, buyers do not need to engage in costly and time consuming contract monitoring activities. Whether contractors are functioning in a cost effective fashion or not is irrelevant. To them the bottom line is that they will be delivered goods and services that meet their requirements at an agreed upon price, regardless of the cost of the effort to the contractor.

While contractors bear the brunt of contract risk on firm fixed price contracts, we have already seen that high performing contractors can earn substantial margins on them if they are innovative and well managed.

DISADVANTAGES OF FIRM FIXED CONTRACTS

The possible disadvantage of firm fixed price contracts to contractors is obvious: if the effort encounters cost overruns, they may cause the contractor to experience losses.

Even buyers need to be sensitive to the risks they face with this seemingly low risk approach, because if contractors get in trouble and begin hemorrhaging financially, they may be tempted to cut corners. This means the buyer will receive an inferior deliverable. The troubled contractors may even go out of business, in which case buyers receive nothing for their outlays.

FIXED PRICE WITH REDETERMINATION

It is common to have escalation clauses included in some contracts with long delivery times, such as construction and production contracts. These clauses are meant to protect the contractor against cost increases in materials, labor rates, or overhead expenses in economic environments where inflation is a problem. For example, price may be indexed to inflation so that it can be adjusted in the event of inflation. Alternatively, price may be redetermined as costs become known. In this case, the initial price is negotiated with the proviso that it will be redetermined at intervals so that the price can reflect actual cost data.

A variety of redetermination contracts are in use including: those that establish a ceiling price for the contract and permit only downward adjustments; those that permit upward and downward adjustments; and those that establish one readjustment period at the end of the project.

Redetermination contracts are appropriate where engineering and design efforts are difficult to estimate, or in long-term quantity production contracts where the final price cannot be estimated for lack of accurate cost data. Note that the redetermined price may be applied to items already produced as well as future items. A caution to the buyer is that some contractors can abuse redetermination contracts. After negotiating a low price, the contractor may go ahead and produce a few items and then turn round to complain that it has discovered the costs of production to be much higher than expected. The contractor will then ask for price redetermination. In this scenario, the contract has, in effect, become a "cost plus" contract.

UNIT BASED CONTRACTS

A final contract type explored here is the unit based contract. This contract mechanism is employed when dealing with well defined physical goods. The contract may stipulate that in a fixed period of time, the buyer intends to purchase up to 10,000 widgets at $10 each. The contract can be open ended, where no commitment is made to buy a given number of widgets, or it can specify a minimum number of items that will be purchased.

Clearly, unit based contracts are more appropriate in production environments, where physical goods are being produced, than in project environments, which usually have a substantial service component to them that is not amenable to unit based contracting.

SELECTING THE APPROPRIATE CONTRACT TYPE

As indicated at the outset of this book, contracts can be formulated in numerous ways and can contain any imaginable provision, so long as they don't break the law. Theoretically, then, you can choose whatever contract type you want. However, experience shows that smart managers select contract types that fit the circumstances of the work that needs to be done and the environment in which the contract effort is carried out. In this section we offer general guidelines on how to select the appropriate type of contract for the circumstances you face.

In general, work efforts with poorly defined scope are amenable to cost plus contracting. Scope may be ill-defined because work is being carried out in new areas, or technology is continually changing, or the business/social/political environment is dynamic. The point is that circumstances do not allow the SOW, schedule, and budget to be defined in a clear and precise fashion.

When engaging in cost plus contracts, the buyer must be capable of monitoring contractor performance carefully, to make sure that expenses are kept under control. Buyers without such capabilities are inviting cost overruns.

Within the domain of cost plus contracts, CPFF contracts are most appropriate for the least well defined work – for example, on research projects or projects involving the development of new software systems. CPFF projects are generally relatively small development efforts.

CPIF and CPAF contracts are appropriate on larger, more structured projects that still have a strong element of uncertainty associated with them. For example, a $500,000,000 project to upgrade an air traffic control system with the latest technology is likely to be structured in either a CPIF or CPAF format. Whether you adopt the incentive fee or award fee approach depends on circumstances. If you are working with a reliable contractor on a fairly low risk effort, the incentive fee approach works well, because problems of defining target costs accurately and dealing with uncooperative contractors are largely by-passed. If you are working with a contractor who wins an award as a low bidder, or the work effort is uncomfortably ill defined, then a CPAF structure gives you better leverage over the contractor.

Time and materials contracts are appropriate when hiring people to carry out basic services that are not an integral part of a larger, integrated effort. For example, if you suddenly learn that you need to hire a consultant to help in an *ad hoc* marketing effort, it is not necessary to engage in elaborate contracting arrangements – a time and materials contract will do.

FIRM FIXED PRICE CONTRACTS

When scope is well defined, firm fixed price contracts are usually the preferred approach. In general, scope is clearly defined on routine efforts that have been carried out many times before or on complex projects dealing with well-understood technologies and processes. Certainly, purchase of standard goods – such as pencils, office equipment, and widgets – should be governed by firm fixed price contracts.

CHAPTER THREE
SOLICITATION PLANNING

INTRODUCTION

The process of identifying potential suppliers of goods and services requires planning. This process is called solicitation planning. Among other things, it involves the development of the Statement of Work (SOW) and other solicitation documents, such as an RFP, IFB, or RFQ. It entails sending invitations to prospective bidders to submit bids or quotations, depending on the selected procurement mode. Solicitation planning also involves development of criteria that the buyer will use to evaluate bids from prospective contractors.

A misstep at this juncture can be the source of future problems after the contract has been signed and work has begun. Therefore, planning at this stage must be carried out carefully. This chapter discusses what needs to be done to plan for the solicitation effectively.

FULL AND OPEN COMPETITION

There are a number of operating principles in procurement that both buyers and contractors are required to follow. One of them is the *full and open competition principle.* This principle is particularly important in government procurements. It means that every effort should be made by buyers to ensure that the procurement is open to as many qualified bidders as possible, in order to increase competition. It also means that the overall procurement process is conducted fairly. If buyers do not abide by the principle of full and open competition, it may trigger a protest that halts the acquisition process and leads to delays.

While the full and open competition principle must be followed on government acquisitions, well managed for-profit and nonprofit organizations follow it as well. The reason is that this principle reflects good business practice. Without it, acquisitions can be tainted by problems of favoritism and corruption. To the extent that they are not truly competitive, then the buying company is liable to receive inferior goods and services at uncompetitive prices.

Full and open competition is not a blanket principle. There are certain procurement situations where the principle may relaxed. The situations include:

- *Where there is only one qualified source of goods and services.*
  This is called *sole source procurement*. It arises when only one potential contractor has the capability to fill the buyer's needs. This may occur when the contractor is the sole owner of needed technology, or possesses unique skills, or possesses unique data. With sole source situations, it does not make sense to go through the competitive procurement process, since

there are no competitors qualified to bid on the solicitation.

- *Unusual and compelling urgency exists.* This is typically the case where, for example, urgent organizational needs and interests require a speedier approach to contract solicitation. Competitive bidding can be very slow.

- *The terms of an agreement or treaty require the use of specific procedures other than competitive procedures.* The full and open competition principle prevails in industrialized enterprises in the West. However, there are societies that may require procedures that are non-competitive. For example, socialist states may require that contracts be granted to state owned enterprises, even though they are inefficient. Even in Western countries, statutory requirements may demand that contracts be awarded to specific enterprises for assorted compelling reasons. For example, contractors may be forced to offer subcontracts to firms that have security clearances in order to carry out work with national security implications. Or they may be required to award subcontracts to small businesses, reflecting the small business promotion policies of government.

- *Where the use of competitive procedures can result in the disclosure of information that might compromise national interest.*

For the most part, full and open competitive procedures entail making solicitations public. However, when dealing with national security contracts, solicitation documents may contain classified information that the law does not allow to be disclosed publicly.

SOLICITATION VEHICLES

There are various ways that buyers can solicit bids from potential contractors. The three best-known approaches are discussed here: invitations for bid (IFBs), requests for proposals (RFPs), and requests for quotations (RFQ).

INVITATION FOR BIDS (IFB)

IFBs are associated with sealed bidding. Sealed bidding is a method of solicitation that invites competitive bids from prospective contractors. The bids are submitted in sealed envelopes. Public opening of the bids at a specified date, time and place follows the submission of the bids.

Sealed bidding is used for fixed-price contracts. The terms and conditions included in the bid are non-negotiable and represent the bidders *best and final offer* (BAFO). Contracts are usually awarded to the lowest bidder.

IFBs are most appropriate for standard acquisitions that do not entail much customization. Specifications that must be achieved are well defined. Because there is no negotiation of terms and conditions once the sealed bids are open, bidders are under pressure to present an attractive offering, because they will not have an opportunity for further negotiation on terms and conditions with the buyer.

REQUEST FOR PROPOSAL (RFP)

RFPs are associated with negotiated procurements. This form of solicitation is used for non-routine procurements. With negotiated bids, the terms and conditions of the solicitation are negotiable. The objective is to ensure that the buyer's organization obtains the best value. As a result, in addition to price, competitive bidding considers such non-price factors as technical capabilities, past performance of the contractor and the personnel that would be used to do the work. Price is less important with negotiated bids than sealed bids. What this means is that once the best bids have been selected from the lot (the so-called *short list* of finalists), price and other terms can then be further negotiated. The focus on non-price factors in making an award also means that it is possible that an award may go to the high priced bidder.

Negotiated solicitations are initiated through RFPs, which are either advertised in government listings, the trade press or sent directly to lists of potential contractors in the buyer organization's database. Many organizations maintain lists or files with information on prospective contractors, known as qualified seller lists (QSLs).

At the heart of an RFP is the SOW that states the purpose of the RFP and provides a description of the goods and services that the buyer intends to procure from prospective contractors. Following is an outline of a hypothetical RFP that offers "the look and feel" of RFPs as they are formulated in the real world. In practice, there are many variations on how an RFP can be formulated.

Outline of a Hypothetical RFP

1. Introduction
   - Purpose of Solicitation
   - Proposed Form of Contract
2. Description of work
   - Statement of Work (SOW) or SOO
3. Proposal requirements
   - Technical Proposal
     - Name of Contractor's designated Project Manager
     - Qualifications of all professional personnel the contractor intends to be employed by the contractor to do the work

- References: Names, address and telephone numbers of at least three former clients of the contractor
- Subcontracts: If subcontracts are to be used, the contractor must provide a description of each person or firm and the work to be done by each
- Methodology: Contractor shall describe the overall approach to the work, specific techniques to be used, and specific administrative and operational management expertise that will be employed
- Conflict of interest: Prospective contractor must disclose any financial, business, or other relationships that may affect its performance
- Instructions on page headers and numbering
  - Cost proposal
  - Questions: Provides information on the person to whom all questions regarding the RFP should be sent to, the format of the questions and the deadline for the submission of questions
4. Contractor selection – description of the process to be employed by the buyer
  - Technical proposal review
  - Opening of cost proposal
  - Post -award audit of cost proposal

5. General information
   - Proposal submittal: Instructions for submission of proposals, including proposal format, deadline date and to whom the proposal submission should be made
   - Late submittal: Describes conditions under which a proposal would be deemed late and would be returned to the proposer
   - Modification or Withdrawal of Proposals: Specifies conditions governing modification or withdrawal of proposals
   - Public opening of cost proposals: Specifies date for the public opening of cost proposals
   - Schedule of activities relating to the RFP, submission and evaluation of proposals, award of contract, contract commencement date, and contract completion date
   - Property rights: Deals with intellectual property issues relating to a submitted proposal
   - Debriefing: Specifies whether or not debriefing will be provided for unsuccessful proposers
   - Confidentiality
   - Inquiries
   - Notification of right to protest: Specifies the grounds, processes and procedures that proposers may use to protest the award
6. Attachments
   - Sample cost proposal

- Evaluation criteria for technical proposal
- Accounting and audit guidelines
- Standard agreement & proposed agreement language

REQUEST FOR QUOTATION (RFQ)

The RFQ is a vehicle for inviting quotations from prospective contractors who can provide well-defined goods and services that the contractor desires. They are similar to IFBs in that they are useful when attempting to purchase routine items. However, like RFPs, their terms and conditions are negotiable.

PREPARING FOR THE SOLICITATION

The two important activities that an organization carries out as it prepares for a solicitation are the preparation of the solicitation documents (RFP, IFB, or RFQ) and the development of appropriate criteria for the evaluation of bids.

We have already discussed the solicitation vehicles. What we shall add here is that the solicitation documents should be structured to elicit accurate, complete and consistent responses from prospective bidders. If the solicitation documents are poorly articulated and confusing, the response from bidders will be chaotic and off-target. Consequently, the solicitation documents must be clear and easy to understand.

EVALUATION CRITERIA

Criteria employed for assessing the merits of a bid typically address the following areas:

- *Technical merits of proposal*
  Is it internally consistent? Does it reflect good practice? Will the proposed technical solution work? Does the technical solution fully address our needs?

- *Capabilities of individuals to be used for the work*
  Do they have a demonstrable track record of good performance? Do they have the right skills? Will they have the time to work on our project as promised?

- *Organizational capabilities and experience*
  Has the organization successfully executed similar contracts in the past? Does the organization have a reputation for honesty and good work? Are operations managed effectively? Is the management team working on this contract qualified?

- *Effectiveness of work plan*
  Does the work plan make sense? Will it lead to the desired results?

- *Cost effectiveness of financial proposals*
  Does the cost proposal, coupled with the work plan, suggest we will be receiving good value? Is the proposed cost within an acceptable range?

RATING SCHEMES

In principle, the buyer organization can use any rating method it wants to evaluate proposals. Common rating schemes include:

Color Rating
  Blue = Outstanding
  Green = Good
  Yellow = Not acceptable, but correctable
  Red = Not acceptable and not likely to be correctable
Adjectival Ratings
  Outstanding
  Excellent
  Good
  Acceptable
  Unacceptable
Numerical Weights: Proportional score

Technical Merits of Proposal	.40
Capabilities of Individual Performers	.20
Organizational capabilities	.20
Effectiveness of Work Plan	.20
Total	1.0

Numerical Weights: Ordinal Ranking

1st
2nd
3rd
4th

SOLE SOURCE PROCUREMENT

As the term *sole source* implies, there is only one contractor qualified to supply the goods and services desired by the buyer. If this is the case, then there is no need to undergo a competitive procurement. Substantial savings can be realized, because it is not necessary to go through the standard steps of preparing a competitive solicitation and evaluating bids. Sole source solicitations are generally permitted when at least one of the following conditions apply:

- *If the goods or services to be procured were developed at private expense and are covered by proprietary rights.*
  A contractor who controls the patents to a desired technology, or who owns a proprietary data base, or who employs a proprietary production process may be able to argue that it should be awarded a contract on a sole source basis, since no one else is able to supply the required goods or services.

- *If the buyer is responding to an unsolicited proposal.*

A contractor that brings a good idea to the attention of a potential buyer may be able to argue that it should be awarded a sole source contract and avoid competitive bidding, because through its efforts it has made the buyer aware of better ways to conduct its affairs. However, in organizations that strongly pursue free and open competitive bidding, this argument is not likely to hold much water.

- *Procurements that are follow-on to existing contracts*
  It often happens that the initial contract is awarded on a competitive basis and then follow up work is awarded on a sole source basis. The rationale here is that having completed the initial work on a contract, the contractor has developed special knowledge and skills that competitors lack.

54

Chapter Four
Preparing the Bid

Introduction

After a buyer has issued an RFP, IFB, or RFQ, it is now time for potential contractors to review the relevant document and to determine whether or not to bid on the job. If a contractor decides to bid on it, then it needs to organize its proposal development effort. On large bids, this effort is treated as a project in its own right. For example, on large government procurements, the proposal can take more than a year to develop at a cost of millions of dollars.

This chapter examines the processes potential contractors go through when they deal with possible contracting opportunities.

Proposal Development

The process of reviewing an opportunity to bid on a contract and developing a proposal entails a number of standard steps, including:

- Making a bid/no bid decision
- Planning for the proposal development effort
- Attending a bidders' conference
- Using pink team and red team reviews of the proposal

- Producing the proposal
- Reviewing of the proposal document
- Shipping the proposal document to the buyer

MAKING A BID/NO BID DECISION

Proposal writing is a costly undertaken, involving investments of time and money. Given the fact that every investment has an opportunity cost associated with it, it is sound business practice for a firm to assess the benefits and costs associated with a bid before deciding to pursue it. Financial analysis tools such as pay back period analysis and cost/benefit analysis can be of great help in determining the merits of a potential contract business opportunity. The use of these and other tools enables the firm's managers to determine whether it is worthwhile bidding to win a contract.

While the financial merits of a new business opportunity are important, the bid/no bid decision must address a number of other important matters as well. For example: Do we have qualified staff who can work on the contract in the event it is awarded to us? Is the contracted effort in harmony with our corporate culture? Can the contracted effort help us build new capabilities? Will it enhance our reputation?

PLANNING FOR THE PROPOSAL DEVELOPMENT EFFORT

When a decision is made to develop the proposal, the whole effort must be treated as a project and planned accordingly. A proposal-writing leader must be appointed to be responsible for the project – he/she serves as the project manager for the proposal development effort.

The proposal development effort must address a number of things, including:

- *Hold a kick-off meeting to launch the proposal development effort*
  All but the smallest proposals require a team effort. There seldom is enough time to prepare a proposal in a leisurely fashion, so it is important that a team be assembled that can work on the proposal concurrently. Team members need to know their roles and to be able to integrate their efforts into the total effort. Consequently, it is a good idea to launch the proposal writing project with a kick-off meeting, where players are introduced, roles and responsibilities are identified, key objectives are identified, and constraints are defined.

- *Development of an SOW*
  In general, the SOW that will be written for the proposal will strongly reflect the SOW contained in the solicitation document. So if the buyer's SOW states: "Contractor will produce a 25 page technical document," the SOW in the proposal will contain a parallel statement that "Contractor

will produce a 25 page technical document." In preparing the SOW for the proposal, the contractor team must use good sense in articulating SOW elements. For example, if the buyer makes clear that it is looking for creative solutions to problems, then a verbatim repetition of the buyer's SOW will not convey a sense that the contractor can deal with issues creatively. In this case, the contractor needs to figure out how to write a SOW that shows that it is able to be creative in tackling the buyer's problems.

- *Identify resources needed for the effort*
  While thinking through the work needed to satisfy the buyer's requirements, the proposal development team will develop good insights into what resources will be needed to carry out the contracted effort. They must determine the extent to which these resources are available within the organization, and what resources will need to be acquired from outside.

- *Identify and schedule key tasks*
  As the proposal is being developed, key tasks associated with the contracted effort will be identified. The durations and interdependencies of these tasks must be established to serve as the basis of the proposed work plan.

THE PROPOSAL DEVELOPMENT TEAM

Proposals are usually developed with tight deadlines. The proposal development manager must assemble a team of players who can work together effectively and generate a credible proposal with limited information, minimal resources, and little time. Key players on a typical proposal development team include:

- *Proposal development leader*
  Plays the lead role in making sure a credible proposal is produced and submitted on time. This individual serves the function of project manager for the proposal development effort.

- *Sales person/Account executive*
  Usually, the individual who is closest to the customers and who has a good sense of their needs and wants. They provide the proposal development team with customer-focused inputs. Warning: Because sales people are rewarded with commissions, and because their principal goal is to make a sale, they sometimes push to promise more in the proposal than the contractor can really deliver.

- *Project manager for the contracted effort*
  Quite often, a project manager has not yet been identified at this early stage. However, if a project manager has been appointed, his or her input is important because he or she knows what

it takes to do the job. The presence of a project manager in the proposal writing stage reduces the likelihood that the proposal contains promises that cannot be met.

- *Editor*
  Winning proposals need to be put together professionally. They should look good and be error free. The editor's job is to make sure that the proposal document that is ultimately submitted to the buyer reflects high levels of professionalism. Editing a proposal is not an easy job because the document is usually a compendium of cut and paste items that must be brought together and presented seamlessly.

- *Proposal production specialists*
  When you need to produce 30 copies of a 200-page proposal in an afternoon, you appreciate the value of good proposal production specialists. They assemble the document, print it, bind it, pack it, and ship it.

- *Subject matter experts*
  The proposal design and writing team needs to touch base with subject matter experts (SMEs) continually because they possess the substantive knowledge that the buyer is concerned with. Before the proposal is

submitted, it is important that the SMEs do a final reading to check for accuracy of statements.

The bidders' conference (also called contractor conference, vendor conference, and pre-bid conference) is a meeting between the buyer and prospective contractors prior to preparation of proposals by bidders. It is used to ensure that all prospective contractors have a clear and common understanding of the solicitation. Typically, prospective bidders are offered the opportunity to ask questions about the solicitation and to seek clarification on issues. The buyer documents questions and concerns in the conference minutes, which are issued to all bidders.

In lieu of the bidders' conference or even after it, prospective bidders are often allowed to send written inquiries to the buyer within a specified time frame after which no additional inquiries will be entertained. The responses to the inquiries are circulated to all bidders to ensure that no bidder has undue advantage over the others.

When bidders' inquiries prompt revisions to the RFP, copies of the revisions are sent to all prospective bidders. In some cases, the revisions might lead to the extension of the proposal submission date to give prospective bidders time to adjust their proposals in response to the changes.

PINK AND RED TEAMS REVIEWS OF PROPOSALS

These two teams are mechanisms organizations use to strengthen the quality of their proposals. Pink teams are used early in the proposal development effort. Team members come from within the organization, but they play the role of customers reviewing the proposal. They give the proposal development team an outside perspective on how good the proposal is. Red teams are used late in the proposal development effort to critique the almost completed proposal and to help the proposal development team debug the final document and to strengthen it where appropriate.

OUTLINE OF A HYPOTHETICAL PROPOSAL

- *Introduction*
  Demonstrate an understanding of what the customer wants done. Briefly summarize the bidder's experience and organizational capabilities

- *Statement of Work*
  Description of work that will be carried out to produce the defined goods and services

- *Management/Technical Plan (Methodology)*
  Detailed description of steps that will be taken to carry out the work as described in the SOW

- *Organizational Experience/Capabilities*
  Description of the bidder's experience and capabilities that demonstrate that the bidder's organization is qualified to carry out the work as described in the SOW

- *Description of Qualifications of Key Players*
  Resumes of key players who will do the work

- *Price/Financial Proposal*
  An itemized listing of the prices of goods and services offered

- *List of Appendices*
  Supplementary information relevant to the solicitation

PRODUCTION OF THE PROPOSAL DOCUMENT

At this stage the proposal document is put through editorial, legal, and checklist reviews to ensure that it complies with the solicitation requirements and is well written, accurate, and realistic. After these reviews the proposal goes into production.

LETTER OF TRANSMITTAL

A letter of transmittal should be prepared to accompany the proposal. This letter should list the contents of the proposal package, identify the code number of the solicitation (if appropriate) and the name, phone number, and e-mail address of a single point-of-contact in the contractor organization who should be contacted in the event questions arise.

SUBMISSION OF THE PROPOSAL

While shipping a proposal to the buyer is a mundane activity, it is crucially important that it be done right, particularly when submitting a bid by a defined deadline date. Many teams have spent substantial time and money working on writing proposals, only to have their submissions thrown out when they were delivered five minutes beyond the deadline date, or when they were delivered to the wrong office.

Following are some standard rules that bidders should follow when submitting proposals:

- Bids and proposals must be submitted to the buyer in a sealed envelope or package addressed to the office specified in the solicitation, showing the date and time for receipt, the solicitation number, and name and address of the bidder.
- The bidder should request a time-stamped receipt indicating that the proposal was submitted before the deadline date.
- Increasingly, smaller bids can be submitted electronically. This is convenient for both buyer and bidder. However, special care must be taken

to ensure and confirm that the electronic submission was received in accordance with submission requirements.

FIRM BID RULE

This rule affects sealed bids. It states that bids cannot be withdrawn or modified after the public opening. However, sealed bids may be withdrawn or modified, by any method and at any time, before the opening of the bids.

Some organizations that question the integrity of the sealed bid process submit their sealed bids at the last moment in order to forestall leaking of information to competitors.

BUSINESS ISSUES FACING BIDDERS

Up until this point in this chapter, we have taken a "mechanical" view of what bidders go through when responding to solicitations. That is, we have simply described the steps that bidders follow when preparing proposals.

In practice, writing proposals for important contract opportunities is anything but mechanical. In fact, the process can be quite emotional, because different stakeholders in the bidder's organization have different views on the value of the potential contract and how to approach responding to the solicitation.

In this section we examine some important business issues that bidders must contend with, first when making bid/no-bid decisions, then when putting together a winning proposal.

MAKING A BUSINESS CASE WITH LIMITED INFORMATION

Perhaps the most important decision made in the life of a project is whether or not to support it. If an enterprise has infinite resources, it can support all projects. But no enterprise has this luxury. It has finite resources and must be careful to employ them as wisely as possible. Consequently, before deciding to devote resources to writing proposals, smart organizations require that the people favoring a bid response make a business case supporting their views.

The best business cases are those where the bid champions can say unequivocally that if awarded the target contract, the contractor will earn a profit of X dollars, strengthen capabilities in Y and Z technologies, and gain entry into new markets that were previously inaccessible. Beyond this, the best business case should identify the cost of developing the proposal and would reveal the probability of winning the award.

Sadly, it is a rare occasion when sufficient information exists to conduct such an excellent business case. At this stage, the data that is employed in making a business case is based on crude guesswork. The estimates of possible project costs and potential revenues are called *order of magnitude* estimates, or more popularly, *ballpark* estimates. They are usually informed guesses. However, for all the inadequacies of such estimates, it is far better for enterprises to make bid/no-bid decisions based on business cases derived consciously, using informed guesses, rather than depending purely on gut feeling.

PREDICTING THE RESPONSES OF COMPETITORS

When developing proposals, enormous effort goes into trying to calculate how many competitors will submit proposals and then predicting the specific responses of the most formidable competitors. One way to determine who your potential competitors might be is to attend the bidders' conference. At this meeting, you will have a chance to identify potential bidders who are interested in the solicitation. Not all attendees will ultimately bid on the contract. However, you can nonetheless develop a good sense of whether there will be many or few bidders. If representatives from thirty enterprises attend the meeting, and if during the proceeding participants display a keen interest in the solicitation, then you can reasonably deduce that there will be a fairly large number of bidders. This means that your a *priori* chances of winning the contract are fairly low. On the other hand, if only a handful of representatives show up, the a *priori* odds of your winning the award are greater.

Quite often, it is obvious who some of the bidders will be. These are the enterprises who already hold a dominant position in the area covered by the solicitation. Because they have a track record of working successfully in this area, the likelihood of them winning the award is substantially higher than for an average, less experienced bidder.

When the likely bidders have been identified, it becomes important to guess the approach they will take when developing their proposal. Are they a high-cost operation whose bid price will be high? Will they play up their overwhelming dominance of some of the key technologies that will be employed on the contracted project? Will they emphasize their past experience in dealing with the buyer on similar contracts in the past? Can they rely on their brand name to give them an advantage over less known players who may be able to deliver superior products?

Answers to these and other related questions will help you to identify the strategy you should employ in developing your proposal. For example, if the most formidable players are likely to be high-priced bidders, you may decide to compete on the basis of price. Or if they have an established relationship with the buyer, you may emphasize that your enterprise will enable the buyer to take a fresh, innovative approach to dealing with its problems.

The important thing to recognize is that when engaged in competitive bids, no smart player writes a proposal in a vacuum. No one can afford to ignore the bid responses of the other players. Perceptions of the strong and weak points of competitors will have a significant impact on the proposal writing and pricing approach your enterprise takes.

Writing the technical portion of a proposal to carry out a project usually requires a measure of creative thinking. For example, if the project entails developing a next-generation database system, the proposal writing team needs to anticipate future hardware and software developments. It also needs to identify the most effective way that hardware and software can be integrated so as to achieve the buyer's performance requirements in the most effective way.

Even as technical solutions are being mulled over, their schedule and cost consequences must be determined. For example, if an RFP states that a database solution must be developed in a six-month time frame, this requirement dramatically constrains the technical approach that can be taken. It also affects what the project costs will be. In order to determine whether a given solution will be achievable in six months, the proposal writing team needs to identify key tasks that will be carried out on the project, and then to estimate how much time the tasks will consume. Once tasks have been roughly scoped out, it is possible to develop an estimate of the costs associated with executing the tasks.

At the end of this process, the proposal writing team can identify the technical approach the bidding enterprise will take in addressing the project requirements, and can develop schedule and cost estimates for doing the job. It should be noted that while the description of tasks and the estimates of cost and schedule often take on an aura of precision in proposals, they are actually crude guesses. At this stage, the schedule and cost estimates are called *preliminary* estimates. Nonetheless, the bidding enterprise must be careful in presenting its case, because the proposed technical solution and schedule and costs estimates will be transformed into contract promises if the bidding organization receives the contract award.

THE POLITICS OF BIDDING

Business enterprises are not monolithic entities whose employees and managers have a uniform view of the enterprise's priorities and of the courses of action it should pursue. As Bolman and Deal perceptively point out in their book, *Reframing Organizations*, all enterprises have a political dimension to them. They are comprised of coalitions of players with contending needs and wants. The coalitions are comprised of members who band together to achieve desired results. On any given issue, there likely will be two or more coalitions proposing different approaches to dealing with the issue.

This is certainly the case when you consider the views of the managers involved in making a bid/no-bid decision, and among the players providing guidance on how the proposal should be written. For example, during the bid/no-bid decision process, you may find some managers are strongly opposed to dedicating resources to writing a proposal that has little chance of winning an award, while others promote writing the proposal, arguing that the payoffs associated with winning the award are so substantial that they offset the low probability of a win.

One of the thorniest political issues often encountered revolves around the wisdom of writing proposals geared toward "buying the business." What happens here is that those players who are super-eager to win the award (often marketing/sales people) argue that the proposal should promise to deliver as much as possible at an extremely low price. Their point is that if you want to win business in a competitive world, you have no choice but to play this game. Opposed to them are people who say this approach is a recipe for disaster. Who wants to win a contract where you make promises you cannot keep? Often it is the technical players who argue this point. Furthermore, barring miracles, it is likely that the company will lose money on the contract. Does the company really want to pursue money-losing awards?

This conflict is not readily resolved, because both sides have good points. The "buying the business" folks recognize that other bidders are likely to make exaggerated claims about what they can deliver at low prices, and that a company that does not engage in this practice has little chance to win competitive awards. For their part, the "let's be realistic" folks recognize that winning a competitive award may be a pyrrhic victory when it becomes obvious that the promised schedule, budget, and technical performance cannot be achieved, leading to strife with the buyer and likely cost overruns and schedule slippages.

In this book we principally side with the "let's be realistic" crowd. Recent investigations into project failure make it clear that a leading source of failure is unrealistic promises that win business in the short run, but lead to nightmare non-performance situations in the long run. In recent years, buyers have come to recognize that it is not in their interest to have bidders promising to do more than they can actually do, at bargain basement prices. Consequently, the trend has been to move away from making awards on the basis of cost, where contracts automatically go the low bidder, and instead awarding contracts on the basis of best value. Thus if a decision must be made between a bidder that offers to do a job at the lowest cost, and another that offers to do it at a reasonable cost, but with superior performance, then it is justifiable to award the contract to the second bidder because it offers best value.

Having said this, we recognize that even in an era of best value contracts, price is still an important determinant of whether a bidder wins a contract. Consequently, we recommend a compromise approach that bridges the arguments of the two contending sides. We feel that a realistic determination of technical performance, schedule and price should be made initially. Then the enterprise should be willing to make some concessions to the "buy the business" school and provide a modest discount of say five or ten percent in their technical, schedule, and cost promises. This is certainly preferred to the dramatically unrealistic promises that the "buy the business" people usually make. Ultimately, if the enterprise is an innovative, can-do concern, it should be willing to push its people to stretch their capabilities by a few percent in order to win business.

CHAPTER FIVE
SOURCE SELECTION/CONTRACT
AWARD

After proposals have been received, buyers must select a bidder who will be awarded a contract. This process is called *source selection*. The process differs between sealed bid awards and negotiated awards. Source selection for each of these approaches will be discussed briefly.

SELECTION OF A PROVIDER: SEALED BIDS

Sealed bid submissions are submitted in response to solicitations contained in an IFB. Panels of reviewers are employed to examine the merits of the bids that are turned in. The evaluation criteria should be the same as those specified in the solicitation document. Proposed contract prices submitted by all the qualified bidders are compared and analyzed. In general, with sealed bid solicitations, the bid with lowest price is granted the award. However, the panel must determine that the contractor's submission is fully compliant with requirements contained in the IFB, including delivery of goods and services according to a stipulated schedule, and achievement of the specifications.

SELECTION OF A PROVIDER: NEGOTIATED CONTRACTS ARISING FROM RESPONSES TO AN RFP

Under this form of solicitation, each of the proposals is evaluated against the criteria spelled out in the RFP. Usually, technical and financial factors are used to evaluate the proposals. As is the case with sealed bids, a panel of reviewers is used to determine the merits of proposals that are received. After the first round of evaluation, the panel establishes a *short list* of the most attractive proposals.

The source selection process now moves into the negotiation stage. The panel of reviewers negotiates with each of the proposers who lie in the *competitive range*. Every aspect of a proposal is open to negotiation: price, specifications, time frame, technical approach, personnel, and other terms and conditions that can be altered.

In conducting negotiations, both buyer and potential contractor need to assess their relative negotiating strengths and weaknesses. For example, if there are many bidders, the negotiating position of individual bidders is weakened, because the buyer has a substantial pool of players from which to draw. Bidders who do not agree to make concessions are likely to be dropped. On the other hand, if only one credible performer emerges from the competition, its negotiating position is strengthened.

Another example: If the services the buyer desires to acquire are routine, the negotiating position of individual bidders is low, because no bidder possesses an advantage over the others. However, if the desired services require unique capabilities and a creative approach to doing the job, one bidder may stand out from the rest, and its negotiating position is accordingly strengthened.

After the negotiations, each offeror still within the competitive range is allowed to submit a revised final proposal, or *best and final offer* (BAFO). The revised proposals are evaluated by the panel using the source selection criteria specified in the solicitation. A final winner is then selected. It is important that the buyer documents the rationale for the selection in case one of the losers protests the determination. A notification of the award is sent to both the winner and the unsuccessful offerors. At this stage, the buyer and contractor enter into a formal contract.

SELECTION OF A PROVIDER: UNSOLICITED PROPOSALS

Some contractors obtain contracts by submitting proposals to potential buyers outside of the competitive bidding process. They submit unsolicited proposals to potential buyers. While competitive solicitations are being promoted in both government and the private sector, there are many situations where non-competed contract awards may be granted to contractors who submit unsolicited proposals. Examples include:

- Proposals coming from contractors who have unique capabilities to do a particular job (called *sole source* capabilities)
- Proposals coming from contractors that entail contract work that falls below a critical threshold monetary value – on small contracts, the cost of going through a competitive solicitation may be substantially greater than the value of the work that needs to be done
- Proposals coming from contractors who fall into what are called special *set aside* categories – e.g., small businesses, disadvantaged enterprises (e.g., woman-owned, minority-owned) – this is common in the government sector, and may be adopted by government contractors who are required to subcontract a certain portion of their work to companies who qualify for set aside contracts.

With unsolicited proposals, buyers do not sort through a pile of competing proposals. Instead, they work only with the submitted unsolicited proposal and must determine its merits according to their needs, resources, and desire to support the proposed effort. Typically, the department to which the proposal is directed holds an internal meeting to determine whether there is interest in the proposal. If there is, then funding for the possible contract must be identified. This funding might come from within the department or from elsewhere in the organization. If the funds come from within the department, then in most organizations, its managers can decide whether or not to fund a contract.

If they come from outside the department, the proposal likely will need to go through additional review.

Organizations that adhere strictly to competitive acquisitions procedures discourage contractors from submitting unsolicited proposals. One major exception is proposals for sole source efforts, where only one contractor has the needed skills, data, or technology.

CONTRACT NEGOTIATION

The aim of contract negotiations is to allow both the buyer and contractor to reach an acceptable agreement on the terms of the contract through communication and compromise. Negotiations can be emotional, frustrating, difficult, and drawn out, so it is important to strive to keep relations between both sides as cordial as possible. Ultimately, both sides should work to achieve a win-win solution. Occasionally, people approach negotiation from a win-lose perspective – they try to beat down the other side so that they gain nothing. A problem with this approach is that the losing side has little stake in making the agreement work. Although they may sign the contract, it is unlikely that they will take the effort to enable the contract to yield successful results.

In their book *Getting to Yes, Negotiating Agreements without Giving In* (1981), Roger Fisher and William Ury offer the following four principles for successful negotiations:

- *Separate the people from the problems.*

To avoid misinterpretations of actions and statements by the other party, the authors suggest that the contractor should practice empathy by putting itself in the position of the buyer's team to see issues from their point of view.

- *Avoid entrenched positions.*
  Buyers and contractors should avoid being too rigid in holding to their positions. They should look for common ground which can be used as a basis for reaching a win-win solution.

- *Before entering into the negotiations, generate a number of creative options.*
  This is a practical advice. It recognizes that during negotiations, the original positions of buyer and contractor will likely need to change, so both parties should think about acceptable options. It also recognizes that it is difficult to develop creative alternatives during the negotiations owing to the pressure of the negotiation process and in the presence of the other party. To this end, a useful approach is to develop two or three stand-alone technical and financial proposals based on the RFP.
  When developing alternative options, be prepared to trade off tangible for intangible benefits. For example, buyers should be willing to charge less if through the contract they can

develop greater technological capabilities that will generate revenue in the future.

- *Make sure the negotiated solution is tied to mutually agreed upon objective criteria*
Once an agreement is made, it and its rationale should be documented so that conflict does not arise later when the parties hold different views as to what transpired during the negotiation process.
.

MAKING THE AWARD

After the winner has been selected and before a formal contract is signed, it is important for the buyer to satisfy itself that the contractor has the capability of meeting the following standards:

- Has access to adequate financial resources to perform the contract effort.
- Is able to comply with the required or proposed delivery or performance schedule.
- Is qualified to deliver the goods or services specified in the contract.
- Has the administrative capacity to support the contract effort.
- Is not guilty of conflict of interest of any sort.
- Is professionally honest, ethical and trustworthy in its business dealings.

If at this point the contractor still seems qualified to carry out the terms of the contract, then a contract can be written and signed.

FORMAT OF A TYPICAL CONTRACT DOCUMENT

Contract documents can be long or short. For example, contracts for defense acquisitions can be more than one hundred pages long. In contrast, contracts for the delivery of a simple product like office supplies can be one page long. Contracts can also be simple or complex depending on the nature of the solicitation. Furthermore, a contract can be either verbal or written. With oral contracts, nothing is put on paper. Both parties verbally agree on their rights and responsibilities under the contract. A mere handshake can be used to seal the deal and it is binding in law. While this form of contract is simple, an obvious disadvantage is that in the event of a dispute, the plaintiff will have a hard time trying to prove his or her complaint, owing to the absence of documentation.

Our attention here is on the written contract. Typically, written contracts employ the following format:

- *Preliminary statement describing the parties to the contract, when the contract was issued, and the nature of the contract (e.g., firm fixed price, CPFF, CPAF, CPIF, time and materials, unit price)*

This section is straight forward. Contract structure was treated in Chapter 2.

- *The statement of work (SOW)*
  The different approaches to articulating a SOW were described in Chapter 2. A new approach – the performance work statement (PWS) – will be covered in Chapter 9.

- *A description of special conditions that bear on contract performance*
  Many contracts have special conditions that bear on them and must be articulated in the contract document. For example, for work outsourced in China, the contract may contain the following provision: "Employee policies must be carried out in respect to the laws and regulations of the People's Republic of China."

- *A detailed list of deliverables and associated delivery dates*
  This must be determined in the specific context of contracted effort. It is important that no deliverables are accidentally left out, and that delivery dates are realistic.

- *A description of the compensation terms and of how and when payments will be made*
  It is likely that a substantial portion of the final negotiations address compensation terms, i.e., how much money should be paid for the delivery

of different goods and services. The contract
must also stipulate how and when payments will
be paid. For example, will payment be made
after all goods and services have been
delivered? As each item is delivered? Monthly, at
the end of each month? Quarterly? More will be
said on payments in Chapter 6.

- *A detailed description of rights and
  responsibilities of the different parties to the
  contract*
  This portion of the contract makes clear who has
  what responsibilities, e.g., "Buyer will supply
  Contractor with the facilities in which to carry out
  the contracted work"; "Contractor will make sure
  all deliverables, including those coming from
  subcontractors, meet quality standards specified
  in Paragraph 22, Section C.3 of this document."

- *A description of intellectual property rights*
  In view of the importance and value of
  intellectual assets, it is crucial that treatment of
  intellectual assets employed during the course of
  the contract or emerging from the contractual
  effort be treated clearly and forcefully. For
  example, if the contractor employs its proprietary
  database to carry out contract work, it should
  specify that it retains full control over it. If as a
  consequence of the contractor's work a new
  database emerges, buyer should stipulate that it

has complete rights over the newly created database.

- *A description of penalties associated with poor performance (or possibly bonuses associated with superlative performance)*
  Schedule delays typically carry financial penalties. Poor quality goods and services will not be accepted and paid for – in addition, penalties may be levied for poor quality work. Occasionally, buyers will hire another party to correct deficiencies and *charge back* to the original contractor the costs of the corrective work.

- *A description of how the contract can be terminated*
  A contract can stipulate a variety ways that it can be terminated, including: goods and services have been satisfactorily delivered; a defined period of time has passed; one or both parties want to terminate it without cause (advanced notice is usually required); the buyer wants to terminate it because of poor contractor performance; the contractor wants to terminate it because the buyer makes it impossible for it to do its job; uncontrollable forces make it impossible to achieve the contract's provisions (this is called *force majeure*, and includes things like floods, fire, and insurrection). Termination provisions should be carefully crafted. On the

one hand, you don't want to make it too easy for the parties to back away from their commitments. On the other hand, you want to make it possible for the parties to have an amicable "divorce" in the event that things simply don't work out between them.

- *Boiler plate items*
  The term boilerplate refers to standard terms, restrictions, and caveats that organizations routinely attach to their contracts. The typical items covered in boilerplate include statements that attest that the contractor:

  o abides by national laws governing occupational safety and health
  o has a surety bond to cover situations where it may not perform its work adequately
  o abides by laws covering environmental quality
  o is an equal opportunity employer
  o will maintain confidentiality in regards to all work performed for the buyer
  o will not represent itself in its dealings as an agent of the buyer
  o will assign intellectual property rights to the buyer for products developed during the course of the contract
  o will apply lower overhead rates when conducting work on the buyer's premises

Protests

The preparation of a proposal can be time consuming and expensive. This is particularly true when bidding on projects, because projects are unique and demand customization in the writing of the proposal. A proposal for a small one person-year effort may take one or two weeks to assemble using the efforts of several people. A proposal for a major public sector project may take a year to prepare at a cost of millions of dollars.

A reality of competitive bids is that you have a winner and one or more losers. The losers have invested time and money in preparing their bids, so if they feel that the award was improperly granted (e.g., published procedures were not followed by the buyer) they might consider protesting it. This is especially true in public sector solicitations, where awards can be very large and where the law requires that they be granted fairly according to well-defined and adhered-to procedures.

Examples of grounds for protest include:

- *Improper evaluation or negotiation.*
  For example, the evaluation panel used an evaluation scheme different from the one stated in the solicitation document. Or the panel did not provide an aggrieved bidder the chance to present revised estimates although the bid was within the competitive range.

- *Improper acceptance of nonconforming proposals or non-responsive bids.*
  Solicitations must be prepared with great care. If five bidders respond to a solicitation and four of them adhere religiously to its instructions and one takes a creative approach that does not, and if the non-conforming one wins the award, the four losers will certainly feel upset and may have grounds to protest the award.

- *Defects in the solicitation.*
  Types of defects include: Incorrect data needed in order to respond to the solicitation; incorrect instructions on procedures that should be followed in writing the proposal, including formatting instructions, deadline dates, length of response; poorly formulated SOW.

- *Failure to supply the bidder with amendments to the solicitation*
  A bidder who has not received amendments to the solicitation that were provided to other bidders may have grounds for protest.

- *Improper restrictions on competition.*
  A common complaint on public sector solicitations is that they have been "wired." That is, the solicitation is so restrictive that only one company can bid on it – the company that the government client wants to select.

Most large organizations have mechanisms to handle protests. The procedures define on what grounds protests can be made and the steps complainants must follow to lodge a protest. When protests are registered, the first action is to determine whether they qualify for review by addressing their merits. If they qualify, then the complaint must be examined and a determination must be made as to its merits. Procedures like this can add substantially to the amount of time it takes to grant an award. Clearly, it is important for the buyer to conduct the whole solicitation process transparently and according to the rules of engagement specified in the solicitation vehicle. A court may uphold a protest if it finds the buyer's award decision to be irrational, arbitrary and capricious.

CHAPTER SIX
CONTRACT ADMINISTRATION

Once a contract has been signed, work can begin on it. At this point, contract administration becomes the focal point of activity in the procurement process. Contract administration focuses on ensuring the effective and efficient execution of the contract. It encompasses all activities that need to be undertaken by both the buyer and the contractor or their appointed representatives to ensure that the contractors meet their performance, delivery and cost obligations.

The nature of the contract administration effort is colored by the contract type. With fixed price contracts, the administrative burden on buyers is reduced, because their principal concern is to get the deliverable on time, at a negotiated price, and according to the specifications. They are not concerned – at least in theory – whether the effort is facing a cost overrun, because the burden of cost overruns is assumed by the contractor.

With cost reimbursable contracts buyers must have effective contract monitoring procedures in place, because the money the contractor is spending is *their* money. Each penny of non-allowable expense or cost overrun comes out of *their* pockets.

A contract imposes certain administrative duties and responsibilities on both the buyer and the contractor. This chapter looks at the duties and responsibilities of buyers and contractors in contract administration. It also addresses other pertinent issues, including: contractor performance monitoring, change control, contract disputes and resolution and relationship management.

ROLE OF THE BUYER IN CONTRACT ADMINISTRATION

The basic functions of contract administration are fairly constant across organizations, although the specifics can vary substantially. For example, in the US Federal Government, the contract administration function is spelled out in detail in the *Federal Acquisition Regulations* (*FARs*). The *FARs* identify key players in contract administration, including Contract Officers (COs), Contract Officer's Representatives (CORs), and Contract Officer's Technical Representatives (COTRs). In the private sector, contract matters are usually run out of a contracts or procurement office. Non-standard contract documents are formulated by attorneys and administered by contract specialists. Standard documents may be handled entirely by contract specialists.

In this chapter, we talk about the role of the contract office, recognizing that different organizations implement the contract management effort in different ways.

There are four fundamental functions carried out by contracts offices as part of the contract administration process: document management; performance monitoring; inspection, acceptance, and quality control;

and payment for work done. Each of these functions will be discussed in some detail.

DOCUMENT MANAGEMENT

The need for proper records keeping in procurement management is strong. The buyer should be able to track all of its actions in respect to its contracts. It needs to know what it has authorized the contractor to do, what contract provisions have been changed, what contractor generated requests it has handled, and so on. Well kept documentation is helpful in the event of disputes between the buyer and contractor.

Contracts offices must keep a file for each contract and contractor. Copies of the contract itself, solicitation documents, and all changes, addenda or supplements to the original contract must be kept in this file. Other documents to be kept include all internal review and approval documents, contractor status report sheets, quality assurance documentation, financial and cost accounting records, pay administration records, minutes of meetings with the contractor, change requests and approvals, acquisition and supply records.

PERFORMANCE MONITORING

The contract office has ultimate responsibility to determine whether the contracted work is being achieved in accordance with contractual provisions. Of course, the contract specialists assigned to monitor contracts lack the substantive knowledge and skills to make this determination alone. Consequently, they must work closely with knowledgeable colleagues within their organization. One obvious candidate is the customers within the organization for whom the contracted work is being done. In particular, if one customer plays a lead role in working with the contractor, this individual should regularly inform the contract specialist about the performance status of the contracted work. For example: Is the contractor meeting the SOW requirements? Is it achieving milestones according to the schedule? Without such feedback from their colleagues, contract specialists have little idea of how work is progressing on contracts.

Monitoring chores include:

- *Monitoring progress reports submitted by contractors.*
  The purpose of progress reports is to keep buyers informed about the status of the contract effort. They are usually included as part of the monthly status reports that contractors submit to their clients. They contain information on budget performance (on cost reimbursable contracts) and schedule performance. They describe what physical effort has been accomplished and what issues have surfaced since the last report. If problems are being encountered, they highlight their causes, discuss their implications, and suggest how they can be resolved. Contract specialists work with in-house customers to

review these reports and identify the status of the effort being carried out.

- *Conducting milestone reviews.*
  Well formulated contracts that extend over a period of time usually identify key milestones that should be achieved at specific points in time. Milestone reviews are then conducted to determine whether contract goals – including budget, schedule, and other performance goals – are being achieved in accordance with promises specified in the contract. Milestone reviews serve two important functions. First, they keep buyers informed about the performance of the contractor. Second, they put pressure on contractors to do what they say they will do. Contract specialists work with in-house customers to determine whether milestones are being achieved in accordance with contractual requirements.

INSPECTION, ACCEPTANCE, AND QUALITY CONTROL

An important function of the contract office is to be certain that the work effort and deliverables conform to contract provisions. This is particularly important for payment purposes. If the contractor invoices the buyer for 50 hours of consultant effort expended in March, then the contracts specialist should attempt to determine that 50 hours of effort were indeed carried out.

- *Inspecting deliverables.*
  When the contractor delivers contracted goods to the buyer, the contract office needs to validate that what is delivered conforms to contract requirements. If the contractor delivers 5,000 widgets to the buyer and invoices the buyer $25,000 for the widgets, then the contract specialist should attempt to determine that the widgets conform to contract requirements and that the price charged is the price covered by the contract.

- *Conducting user acceptance tests (UATs).*
  Before the buyer organization accepts deliverables from contractors, the contract office may ask its in-house customers to carry out a user acceptance test (UAT) to make sure that the deliverable performs according to the specifications. If the deliverable does not satisfy the UAT, then the buyer organization will not accept it and pay for it. When dealing with physical products, acceptance tests can take a number of forms. For example, it may entail destructive tests. A destructive test is a type of physical test that requires an end product to be destroyed to determine whether it meets contract standards. Fireproofing and stress tests are common examples of destructive tests. In the

software arena, UATs entail running software programs with live data to make sure they perform as promised.

- *Quality control.* Through inspection and acceptance testing, the contract office is fulfilling a quality control function.

USING STEERING COMMITTEES

We have been talking here about contract specialists working closely with an informed in-house customer to carry out the monitoring, inspection, acceptance, and quality control functions. In some practice areas, steering committees are set up and charged with monitoring responsibilities. These committees are made up of representatives of the buyer and contractor plus other stakeholders. Typically, the contract specialist (or contract officer) will chair the meetings of the steering committee to review the status of the project, to discuss the concerns of both the buyer and the contractor and to make appropriate decisions. It provides a forum for dialogue and exchange of ideas and for handling explosive issues and can promote a cordial relationship between the buyer and contractor.

PAYMENT FOR WORK DONE

Different methods may be used for making payments to a contractor, depending on the nature of the contract. Following are examples of commonly used payment methods:

- *Lump sum payment at conclusion of effort*
  When dealing with simple purchases or short term work efforts, it is common practice to pay for goods or services at one time after they have been completed and/or delivered. For example, if you have contracted a printer to print and bind 200 copies of a report, you settle the total bill after the reports have been produced and delivered.

- *Down payment*
  When the contractor needs to incur substantial out of pocket expenses to produce and deliver something, or if the contractor needs to strengthen a buyer's commitment to purchasing something, buyers may be required to pay a down payment before the contract effort is launched.

- *Pro rata payment*
  On simple contract efforts, buyers may agree to pay contractors on a *pro rata* basis. For example, on a four month contract, they may pay 25% of the bill at the end of the first month,

another 25% of the bill at the end of the second month, and so on.

- *Progress payment*
  With progress payments, buyers pay contractors the value of the effort they have performed or delivered. For example, on a software development project, the contractor may be paid a progress payment for the development of requirements once the requirements have been specified. It may be paid another progress payment once a prototype of the system is developed. And so on. The trick with progress payments is to determine the value of the effort that has been carried out. For example, how do you compute the value of requirements specification or prototype development? The most effective approach to measuring the value of work done is through *earned value management*, a technique geared toward developing work performance measures. Progress payments are commonly used on cost reimbursable contracts. Payments are made to help contractors cover the cost of their work efforts. Frequently, a small percentage of payments (e.g., ten percent) is held back until the work is finally completed.

Role of the Contractor During Contract Administration

As contracts are executed, contractors have a number of obligations to fulfill and chores to carry out. For example, contractors should:

- *Perform work according to the terms of the contract.*
  Contractors must be able to demonstrate that they are making a good faith effort to achieve what they have agreed to accomplish by employing the resources they said they would use, utilizing prescribed materials, managing their vendors effectively, and by responding to the buyer's inquiries.

- *Deliver goods and services defined in the contract in conformity with time, cost and quality standards.*

- *Submit regular and accurate progress reports.*
  Progress reports provide buyers with information about project status. They may also form the basis for invoicing the buyer for work performed. Contracts that involve one-shot supply of a good may not need progress reports. Contracts that entail efforts of some complexity that take place over time require progress reporting. Typically, the contract specifies the format and frequency

of progress report submissions. For example, a contract may require the contractor to submit monthly reports. It is important to note that progress reports are communication tools for the project stakeholders who have keen interest in the project. Many of these stakeholders are busy people. Therefore, it is recommended that a progress report should have the following characteristics:

- Allow readers to grasp quickly the "project pulse"
- Identify issues and propose an action plan to deal with them; and
- Require less than 10 minutes of reading time

- *Submit periodic invoices that are well documented.*
  For example, the invoices should include receipts for materials purchased, evidence of payment to subcontractors, and timesheet data for the work efforts of billable employees.

CHANGE MANAGEMENT IN PROCUREMENT AND CONTRACTING

Changes are commonplace on contracts. Some changes will come from the buyer, some from the contractor, and some will be triggered by conditions in the environment (e.g., regulatory change). These changes will have cost implications. The question arises: Who will pay for them? Change management in contracting is concerned with making sure that the changes that arise are not accidental, and that it is clear who pays for them.

Buyer-driven changes include:

- *the desire for more features*
- *the desire for sexier features*
- *the desire to scale back scope because of a downturn in the market*
- *the desire to scale up scope because of a strengthening of the market*
- *the buyers change their minds about what they really want*

Contractor-driven changes include:

- *the project team develops a better way to do the job*
- *the project team is seeking technically perfect solutions*
- *materials expenses rise and the contractor wants to save money*
- *key personnel leave the organization, so the contractor needs to replace them with people with different qualifications*

Environment-driven changes include:

- *Fire, flood, earthquake or some other natural disaster (force majeure)*
- *Economic, social, or political disruptions on the world scene*
- *Shortages of materials*
- *A key supplier goes bankrupt*
- *Changes in government regulations*
- *Introduction of new technologies*

HANDLING CHANGE REQUESTS

Contract changes are not cost free. On projects, they can have impacts on cost, schedule and quality. Therefore, it is important that the contracting parties agree on a disciplined approach to change management before commencing work.

A disciplined change control process should address who can propose changes, under what conditions, and what procedure should be followed in requesting change. For example, team members on the contractor's side should recognize that they are not authorized to change contract scope, no matter how justified they feel they are in implementing a change. Similarly, players on the buyer's side also should recognize that they are not authorized to demand changes on their own. In many buyer organizations, no changes can be made without the express authorization by the proper player in the contract office, e.g., a contract specialist or a contract attorney.

In following proper change procedures, it is important that all change orders be made and documented pursuant to the change-related clauses in the contract and be in writing, signed, and dated.

Disputes in Contracting

In contracts, different interpretations about who should do what and who should pay for what can arise. It is important that small differences in interpretation are not allowed to escalate into major disputes. The first line of defense against disputes is to formulate contracts clearly. Vaguely phrased contracts are breeding grounds for conflict.

Examples of ambiguous contract requirements that can lead to trouble include:

- "Contractor will paint the room a pleasing color of beige." (What's "pleasing"? What type of paint should be used? What portion of the room should be painted?)
- "Contractor will deliver the reports to buyer as quickly as possible." (The lack of a specific deadline date will certainly create problems.)
- "Contractor will use whomever they need to carry out the task." (Many people or few? Shouldn't some statement of qualifications of employees be made?)

But even well formulated contracts have their share of disputes. This section examines some common sources of disputes and approaches that can be taken to resolve them.

SOURCES OF DISPUTES

The sources of disputes appear limitless. Only a handful are addressed here.

SCOPE CHANGES

One of the most common sources of disputes is scope change, which can be triggered by either buyer or contractor. As we saw above, buyers might change their minds on what they want contractors to deliver. Or the contractor's technical team members may decide to change the design of the deliverable in order to incorporate the latest technology.

Uncontrolled scope change creates a number of problems. The most obvious is: Who pays for the costs associated with making the changes? The answer is not always obvious. Buyers, for example, may feel strongly that their change requests are minor and fall in the realm of reasonable requests for adjustments that are inevitable on contracts. Contractors may view these same requests as an attempt by the buyer to get something for nothing.

Another example: Quite often, the specifications for a deliverable that are contained in a contract are not completely on target. Consequently, one party might think they need to be adjusted. Yet the other party might not. So how should the issue be resolved?

Perhaps the most serious consequence of scope change is when the modification causes undesired changes in the nature of the deliverable. What began as an effort to create a horse evolves into an endeavor to develop a camel. Not only are there issues as to who pays for the change – questions on the physical integrity and usefulness of the final deliverable arise as well, as do concerns about delays in performing the work effort.

UNAUTHORIZED WORK

A special case of scope change arises when someone in the buyer organization who is not authorized to request changes makes such a request nonetheless, and the contractor complies with it. This can be a tricky matter to resolve. The contractor can argue that it was reasonable to assume that the person making the request was authorized to do so, particularly if that person was "the customer" who was applying substantial pressure to implement the change. The buyer can counter that the contractor should know the rules, and that only change requests blessed by the contract specialist are legitimate. When these types of disputes go to court, the final rulings can go either way since both arguments have a measure of merit.

UNREALISTIC DEMANDS ON THE CONTRACTOR

On occasion, buyers who believe they have a strong bargaining position use their strength to impose unrealistic demands on the contractor. Contractors who eagerly seek new business may agree to comply with these demands so as not to lose business.

Experience shows that this scenario often evolves into a lose-lose proposition. Contractors may find that they simply cannot keep their promises, putting them into a default position. Consequently, buyers may find that they are unable to get what they want in a timely way.

POOR SERVICE DELIVERY

Buyers often complain that in order to win contract awards, their contractors promise more than they can deliver. Once the contract is underway, it becomes obvious that the contractors will not be able to meet the contract requirements, and this creates contract problems.

Another service delivery problem that is often encountered is when contractors deliver defective deliverables. For example, a software system delivered to a client might be bug-ridden, rendering it marginally usable.

OVER-CHARGING

Over charging for contract services and goods can occur in a number of ways. For example, on cost reimbursable contracts, expenses and services can be padded. This is why it is important that the contracts office validate expenses that contractors want reimbursed. Another example: The contractor may charge the client for engaging in a development effort to produce something that has already been produced on another contract.

HANDLING CONTRACT DISPUTES

Buyers and contractors should recognize that disputes may arise on the contract and that they need to be able to deal with them. There are various ways that disputes can be handled, ranging from attempts at resolving them amicably through discussion and compromise to nasty and costly litigation. Ideally, disputes are handled amicably. In reality, however, it may be necessary to resolve them in a more structured and forceful fashion.

This section discusses some of the more commonly employed procedures for handling contract disputes.

PRECAUTIONARY MEASURES

The incidence of contract disputes can be minimized if certain precautionary measures are taken. Included here are:

- Perform an extensive background check on the contractor's references, history, and finances to confirm its credentials before signing the contract document. (This process is called *due diligence*.) It is usually helpful to contact former clients and employees of the contractor.
- Make sure the language of the contract is clear, concise and complete. Take steps to remove ambiguous statements.
- Insert alternative dispute resolution mechanisms in the contract to allow for out of court settlement in the event serious disputes arise.
- If you outsource your software development, make sure your vendor has the right to use the software it will be embedding in its solution. You don't want to discover later that the software you paid for includes copyrighted work that is being used illegally. Negotiate an indemnity clause into the contract, investing the vendor with the full responsibility for any third-party claims (e.g., copyright infringement claims).
- Formulate realistic contractual terms to avoid placing unrealistic demands on the contractor
- Have a testing procedure written into the contract to determine whether an acceptable product has been delivered.
- Build in financial incentives for early delivery and penalties for late delivery.

- Ensure that all communications with the contractor and its team members are clear, concise and unambiguous.
- Have a well-crafted, properly communicated and understood change control policy in place. Document and monitor all changes to the scope of the contract.
- Religiously organize project-status meetings once a week to review contract status.

LITIGATION

Almost everyone agrees that disputants should turn to litigation as a course of last resort. The problem is that it can be acrimonious, expensive, and disruptive.

Despite its unattractiveness in many situations, disputants still resort to it frequently. Its appeal is evident in a number of situations, including:

- when very large sums of money are involved
- when an aggrieved party wants to punish another party
- when one party refuses to settle an issue
- when one party is clearly in the wrong and has damaged the other party

MEDIATION

With mediation, the parties to a dispute attempt to see if they can resolve their differences without having a solution imposed on them by an outside force (e.g., a judge). Typically, an objective, third-party mediator helps facilitate the discussion between the contending parties with a view of seeing what views they hold in common. Mediation works well when the parties are looking for a fair resolution to their problems or when the parties are concerned about the expense and hassle of more formal legal proceedings. It does not work well when there are irreconcilable difference between the contending parties, and one wants to punish the other.

ARBITRATION

With arbitration, contending parties agree to argue their points before an objective, third party arbitrator. After hearing the arguments of the two sides, the arbitrator renders a judgment. With binding arbitration, the contending parties agree to abide by the arbitrator's judgment. With non-binding arbitration, acceptance of the arbitrator's judgment is voluntary.

RELATIONSHIP MANAGEMENT

There is general agreement that contractual conflicts tend to be far more acrimonious than necessary. A significant source of acrimony is that the parties do not know how to deal with each other in a civil, meaningful way. Each side tends to demonize the other. Instead of communicating concerns with each other, barriers to communication are erected.

Clearly, dealing with root causes of conflict and opening communication between the conflicting parties may help resolve disputes before they escalate into full-blown legal battles. Common sources of people-focused disputes between contractors and buyers include:

- personality conflicts
- cultural differences (e.g., engineering vs. business culture)
- conflicts over contracting procedures
- lack of trust (e.g., buyer sees contractor as greedy and unprincipled; contractor sees buyer as constantly trying to get something for nothing).

MANAGING CONFLICTS ON CONTRACTS

In projects, conflict may erupt between the buyer and the contractor or between the contractor and subcontractors. A whole literature exists on managing conflicts and courses have been developed at universities and training companies to help managers learn to identify and handle conflict. Because the potential for conflict exists on the majority of contracts, it behooves key players in the contractor and buyer organizations to familiarize themselves with current thinking on conflict management and to strive to develop skills to handle conflicts when they arise.

CONTRACT CLAIMS

Occasions arise when either party to a contract – buyer or contractor – may feel that it has incurred extra costs or losses owing to an improper implementation of the contract. In this case, the aggrieved party may submit *contract claims* to the other party. The formal definition of a contract claim is:

Any request for relief, adjustment, or consideration by a party to the contract for an act which, in the opinion of the claimant, is not within the scope of intent of the original contract.

US Office of Personnel Management
US Federal Government

Consider the following frequently encountered scenario for a claim: A contractor feels that it has been asked by the buyer to do more work than required by the contract's statement of work. This extra work has cost it $45,000 in extra expenses. What the contractor can do is to file a claim for the $45,000 with the buyer's contracting office. The filed claim should describe the justification for the $45,000 charge. In addition, it should contain a statement signed by a senior manager from the contractor's organization indicating that this claim is being made in good faith – i.e., it is not a frivolous claim.

A contract officer from the buyer's contract office examines the claim to see whether it has merit. He/she issues a statement indicating his/her judgment. If the contractor finds the judgment to be satisfactory, the issue is resolved. If it is viewed as unsatisfactory, then it needs to be resolved in accordance with the contract resolution approaches described earlier in this chapter.

CHAPTER 7
CONTRACT CLOSE OUT

Contracts end in one of three ways. First, contracts come to an end after all the conditions contained in them have been satisfied. In this case, all required goods and services have been delivered by the contractor and accepted by the buyer. For example, if a contractor has successfully installed a new database system, as specified in a contract, the contract can be concluded. This is a happy ending!

Second, contracts may be brought to an end by mutual agreement of the parties, who concur that it is best to close out the contract because it is not able to achieve its goals. This may happen, for instance, when technological change causes an item being developed by means of a contract to become obsolete.

Third, a contract may come to an end because of an act of breach of contract by one of the parties. This is an unhappy situation and may lead, eventually, to legal struggles as both parties try to work out who has what obligations, and who owes what to whom.

In this chapter, we only address the first scenario described above, where a contract ends on a happy note. Our focus is therefore on activities that have to be undertaken to signify the official closeout of the contract.

Contract close out involves two key activities: customer acceptance and administrative closeout. Each of these activities will be discussed briefly.

CUSTOMER ACCEPTANCE

When the contract effort is done, customer acceptance has to be obtained before final payments are made and the contract is closed out. Customer acceptance offers *prima facie* evidence that the contractor has successfully completed the work. Problems arise when the customer rejects the completed work. In this case, the contract will not be closed down until acceptance is achieved. This may mean that the contractor has more work to carry out. An important question that arises here is: If more work needs to be done to produce an acceptable deliverable, who pays for the additional effort? If the additional work is a consequence of new requirements created by the buyer, then the buyer is expected to pay. However, if the additional work reflects deficiencies in the deliverable rooted in poor contractor work, then the contractor is expected to pay. An example of this is the *charge back*, where a dissatisfied customer has another contractor remedy deficiencies in the deliverable and charges the extra expenses back to the contractor.

Customer acceptance can be gained in various ways. For example, customers may carry out a customer acceptance test (CAT), also referred to as a user acceptance test (UAT) in the information technology arena. This test puts the deliverable through its paces to ascertain whether it is performing to specifications. Or customer acceptance may involve less formal customer walkthroughs or inspections of sample deliverables. If the buyer's representatives are satisfied that work has been completed according the terms of the contract, the contractor turns over the final deliverable to the buyer. The buyer in turn formally notifies the contractor that the contract has been completed. This means that the contractor is relieved from further responsibility except in three circumstances:

- *Latent defects*, in which a defect exists at the time of the inspection but is not discoverable through reasonable inspection.
- *Fraud*, which carries criminal connotations, and where the contractor's intent is to deceive the buyer.
- *Warranties*, which continue for a specified time from the date the buyer issues the formal letter of acceptance.

ADMINISTRATIVE CLOSEOUT

After customer acceptance is achieved, the contract is brought to closure by means of administrative actions. These include:

- The buyer prepares a certificate of completion or conformance and then issues a contract completion notice to the contractor.
- The buyer prepares a closeout report.
- People and equipment employed on the project are reassigned.

117

- The buyer makes final payment to the contractor.
- The buyer carries out a lessons learned exercise and archives its conclusions.

Actions by the contractor include:

- Ensures that it receives a contract completion notice from the buyer.
- Prepares a closeout report that carefully documents lessons learned.
- Submits all final invoices to the buyer and ensures that it gets the final and all other outstanding payments from the buyer.
- Ensures it obtains release of performance bonds and letters of credit.

CHAPTER 8
ODDS AND ENDS

Anyone running a business must learn to handle a plethora of contracts. When you hire a new employee, you and the employee sign an employee contract that defines the terms of the hiring arrangement. You may also have the employee sign a non-disclosure agreement to protect your intellectual assets, as well as a non-competition agreement. Meanwhile, the order processing and accounting software you use is likely made available to you through a licensing arrangement. And so it goes.

This chapter briefly reviews a range of contracts and contract provisions that managers frequently encounter as they conduct their regular business affairs. Some can be written as boiler plate documents – for example, standard non-disclosure, non-competition, and copyright assignment agreements can be developed. Others need to be customized to deal with specific circumstances – for example, while the basic outline of licensing agreements and employment contracts can be developed as templates, substantial work must be carried out customizing the details to deal with specific circumstances.

The contractual arrangements covered here are:

- Subcontracting.
- Employment contracts.

- Non-competition agreements.
- Non-disclosure agreements.
- Intellectual property agreements.
- Licensing agreements.

Each of these contractual arrangements will be discussed briefly.

SUBCONTRACTING

This book has focused so far on straight forward contracting between a buyer and contractor. In this section, we briefly examine the situation where contractors subcontract a portion of their work to subcontractors.

For the most part, the same principles and practices of contracting apply to subcontracting, since subcontracts are contracts. Only now the contractor plays the role of buyer in respect to the subcontractors. In hiring subcontractors, the contractor goes through the standard steps encountered by all buyers: solicitation, making an award, and administering and monitoring subcontractor performance in the post-award phase.

While subcontracting entails employing the same principles and practices described in the previous chapters of this book, two features unique to subcontracting need to be highlighted: first, failure of a subcontractor to perform adequately does not absolve the contractor from meeting its contractual responsibilities to the buyer; and second, owing to the legal principle of *privity*, buyers need to be careful about what stipulations they place on contractors in regard to the contractors' dealings with their subcontractors. Each of these issues will be discussed in turn.

FAILURE OF SUBCONTRACTORS TO PERFORM ADEQUATELY DOES NOT ABSOLVE CONTRACTORS FROM MEETING THEIR CONTRACTUAL RESPONSIBILITIES

When contractors enter into contracts with buyers, they are required to meet the terms and conditions of the contract regardless of the performance of their subcontractors. Thus they must monitor subcontractor performance carefully. If subcontractors encounter schedule slippages, they must be sure this does not affect the schedule of the overall project. If subcontractors are unable to meet the specifications for the deliverable, the contractor must figure out what actions need to be taken to achieve the specs (e.g., hiring another subcontractor to complete the work).

While there are many possible reasons for poor subcontractor performance, two stand out. First, when subcontractors are small businesses, they face a number of challenges that larger, more stable enterprises do not. For example, in the event that technical problems arise, they may lack a depth of resources to fall back on (e.g., additional engineers who can be assigned to the subcontract). Another example: if a problem arises elsewhere in the company, this may have negative impacts on being able to perform adequately on the subcontracted work efforts (e.g., resources may be pulled off the subcontracted work to cover the problems faced elsewhere).

Second, if the subcontracted work effort is relatively small, it may not receive the attention it deserves by the subcontractor. This problem is commonly encountered when dealing with larger subcontractors who have a substantial backlog of work. The small job gets lost in the shuffle.

BUYERS NEED TO BE CAREFUL ABOUT WHAT CONDITIONS THEY IMPOSE ON CONTRACTORS IN RESPECT TO SUBCONTRACTOR EFFORTS

In contract law, the term *privity* refers to the legal relationship established between two parties. When a buyer enters into a contract with a contractor, that establishes a privity relationship between the buyer and contractor. When in turn a contractor enters into a contractual arrangement with a subcontractor, that establishes a privity relationship between the contractor and subcontractor.

Buyers must be careful about what conditions they place on contractors in respect to how contractors deal with their subcontractors. If they become too prescriptive and subcontractors fail to meet their obligations, contractors can argue that the buyers' meddling with subcontractor performance contributed to the subcontractor's failure. If this can be demonstrated, then it may absolve them of responsibility for meeting contract terms affected by the buyers' intrusion. In a sense, by establishing overly prescriptive requirements on subcontractors, buyers have established a privity relationship with them, by-passing the privity relationship between the contractor and subcontractor.

The best policy for buyers to pursue is to be clear about what requirements the contractor must meet, and to shift the burden of meeting these requirements onto the contractor. For example, if on large projects the contractor must provide monthly earned value management reports detailing cost and schedule status for project work, then buyers should avoid the temptation to require explicitly that contractors impose earned value reporting requirements on their subcontractors. They do not need to do this! It is likely that the contractors will on their own impose earned value reporting requirements on their subcontractors so that they can meet their obligations as spelled out in the contract.

EMPLOYMENT CONTRACTS

Employment contracts define the general terms of an individual's employment with an organization, identifying the responsibilities of the organization and employee to each other and describing the relationships of the two parties under various conditions. Following are some standard items covered in employee contracts for executive level employees.

- *Term of employment and compensation*
  This section defines the general nature of the job, the length of employment and salary.

- *Extension*
  This section describes how the contract will automatically be extended for a defined period of time in the event that the original contract runs its course and both parties would like to continue the contractual arrangement.

- *Working facilities*
  When dealing with senior executives, it may be important to specify the type of office environment they will work in. Also, it is important to specify working facility arrangements for employees who work out of their homes or who spend substantial time on the road.

- *Expense reimbursement*
  Managers who engage in substantial travel, or who entertain clients heavily, will want an employment contract to be clear about arrangements to reimburse them for their expenses. This portion of the agreement should also specify what the "allowable" expenses are.

- *Benefits*

  Most employees receive a range of non-salary benefits in addition to their salaries. The employment contract should specify what these benefits are. Typical benefits include:

  - Medical insurance
  - Life insurance
  - Vacation/sick days
  - Bonus
  - Pension plan

- *Termination and dismissal*

  Provisions must be made for the situation where employment ends earlier than specified in the employment agreement. Typical circumstances that should be covered include:

  - poor performance by the employee
  - death of the employee
  - physical or mental incapacity of the employee
  - dishonest behavior on the part of the employee

  Beyond this, the employer may add a provision that it has to right to terminate the employment agreement without cause. Provisions for severance payments may be included. The amount of payment will depend on a number of factors. For example, regular employees doing standard jobs may be given two months of severance pay. Senior executives may require contracts that provide them with substantial severance pay (so-called Golden Parachutes).

The agreement should also stipulate under what conditions the employee can terminate employment. Again, routine workers may be asked to provide two weeks of notice prior to leaving the enterprise. Other employees who have special skills or who are senior executives may be asked to provide longer lead times.

- *Restrictive covenants*
  Employment agreements usually have provisions restricting what the employee can do, e.g., he or she cannot offer services to a competitor, cannot provide confidential information to anyone outside the employing organization, cannot work in competition with the employer for a period of more than one year after termination of employment.

- *Indemnification*
  A provision where the employer agrees to cover legal expenses that might arise in the event the employee is sued in connection for actions that he or she undertook as part of his or her duties toward the employer.

- *Severability*
  A provision that states that if for whatever reason a portion of the agreement cannot be enforced, the remainder of the agreement is still in effect.

Non-Competition Agreements

It is common practice today to have employees sign an agreement stating that they will not engage in activities that will lead them to compete against their employer's business for a fixed period of time after termination of their employment with the employer. For example, someone who has built the operations department of a software firm that specializes in developing unique order processing software may be proscribed from engaging in similar business for a period of two years after leaving the employer.

The principal issue with non-competition agreements is their enforceability. The agreement is likely to be enforceable in the case of employees who develop unique, high-value, specialized skills because of their association with the employer, particularly if competition by the employee can measurably hurt its business prospects. On the other hand, restrictions on employees' future employment is not likely to be enforceable if they are working in non-unique areas. For example, an employer will not be successful in enforcing an agreement where a delivery truck operator has agreed not to work as a delivery truck driver with other companies for a period of two years after leaving the employer. Similarly, a university cannot seriously expect a history professor to stop teaching history for a period of one year after leaving the university.

In writing non-competition agreements, the employers' guiding principle should be to make sure that the restrictions they place on their employees' future employment opportunities are reasonable. In general, provisions that deny a worker a means of livelihood are not enforceable.

One approach to assure that a non-competition agreement is enforceable is to offer employees money in exchange for signing the non-competition agreement. For example, a major training company paid its senior executives $100,000 to sign a non-competition agreement, where they agreed not to compete against the employer for a period of two years after leaving the company. Because they received compensation for signing the non-competition agreement, it became unambiguously enforceable.

Non-Disclosure Agreements

Employees, including contracted workers, are often required to sign a non-disclosure agreement with their employers. These agreements are often configured to deal with two types of situations. In one, the terms of the agreement protect the employer's intellectual assets and business strategies, including such things as trade secrets, business development strategies, business plans, and customer mailing lists. In the other, the agreements are designed to protect the privacy of individuals – for example, clients and fellow employees.

An important issue often encountered with non-disclosure agreements is that if the employee breaks them, the damage has been done. For example, once a trade secret is revealed publicly, it loses its value. In this case, the employer can take the employee to court, but it is unlikely that the full value of the lost asset can be restored.

INTELLECTUAL PROPERTY AGREEMENTS

If Person A pays Person B to write an original piece of work, then under most circumstances the law recognizes Person A's right to own the work, since it is viewed as a *work for hire*. In order to strengthen its legal position, the smart employer has employees (including contracted workers) sign a copyright assignment agreement, where employees acknowledge that any work created on behalf of the employer is owned by the employer.

The same principle applies to patented technology. Once again, the smart employer has employees (including contracted workers) sign a patent assignment agreement, where employees agree to sign over the rights to inventions made on the job to their employer.

Having copyright and patent assignment agreements are particularly important in a number of areas are ownership of intellectual assets can be fuzzy.

For example, volunteer organizations that use volunteers to write professional standards cannot rely on *work for hire* principles, since the volunteers are not being paid for their work. If these organizations want to maintain control over their intellectual assets, they should have volunteers sign copyright assignment agreements at the outset of their work efforts. (In practice, volunteers sometimes resist this request, arguing that they should be able to keep whatever they produce if they are not being paid for their travails.)

In recent years, universities have had research professors sign patent assignment agreements. Historically, professors have felt entitled to keep ownership over the products of their intellectual efforts. However, their arguments do not hold much water when their successes result from investments made by universities into lab equipment and the salaries of researchers, graduate assistants, and additional support staff. In order to be clear about the ownership of the products of an academic research effort, universities should require their professors to agree to provide ownership rights of the inventions they develop to the universities.

On projects using contractors, the matter of ownership rights of intellectual assets can be maddeningly ambiguous, so it is important that these be spelled out clearly. For example, when a contractor employs its own proprietary data to conduct an analysis for a customer, and the analysis yields additional data that is closely tied to the original data, who owns the derived data? Disputes on who owns what arise frequently on contracts, and the best way to avoid conflict – and possibly litigation – is to deal with ownership matters carefully in the contract document.

Licensing Agreements

A license is an agreement between a licensor and a licensee, where the licensor agrees to allow the licensee use its property under controlled circumstances.

Licenses appear in many formats. For example, when customers buy commercial software packages, they often encounter a statement that says that by breaking a seal on the package, they are agreeing to the terms of a license that is written in small print on the side of the package. The point here is that the purchaser of the software package is *not* its owner, but is a licensee who has purchased use of the software for a fee. The small print describes the conditions under which the purchaser can employ the software.

Other ways that licenses can be used include:

- Licensing use of course material to be taught by a training company
- Licensing a process employed in manufacturing
- Licensing use of a trademark
- Licensing a trade secret
- Licensing patented technology

There are several reasons why licensors and licensees enter into licensing arrangements. From the licensees' perspective, they can access existing technology without having to re-invent it, they can save on R&D costs, they can employ the licensed technology to increase their technological capabilities, they reduce the risk of new product development by licensing tried-and-true technology, and so on. From the licensors' perspective, they can help pay back R&D costs through the licensing royalties they earn, they can use the license to establish relations with new partners, they can have licensees sell back products produced under license at a price that is lower than their own production costs, and so on.

As mentioned earlier, with licenses, licensors provide licensees use of their property under controlled circumstances. The controls take various forms. Typical restrictions included in licensing agreements are:

- *Territorial restrictions*
  The licensee can produced goods and services under license for distribution in a clearly demarcated territory.

- *Restricted quantity of production*
  The licensor may impose a restriction on the quantity of goods a licensee can produce.

- *Tying in provisions*

The licensee is required to obtain certain materials and spare parts only from the licensor.

- *Package licensing*
  To obtain the desired license, the licensee is required to license additional technology that it may not want.

- *Quality control restrictions*
  A licensor who allows licensees to produce goods and services that bear its trademark will want to impose strict quality control measures on the licensee, since shoddy products will ruin its reputation. Occasionally, licensees resist these measures, arguing that the licensor's quality control demands are interfering with their business operations.

Licensing agreements establish the terms of payment by which the licensee pays the licensor. There are many ways payment can be made, including:

- lump-sum payment
- royalties based on percentage of revenues associated with sales of products produced under license (e.g., 5% of gross revenues)
- royalties based on the number of units of goods sold
- down payments before the licensing agreement is launched

- buy-back provisions (where the licensor can buy back products at a low price)
- equity share in the licensee organization

Individuals and entities entering into licensing agreements should be aware that the effective management of licensing requires great care. Licensors should be prepared to have processes in place to monitor the licensee's use of the licensed technology. For example, if the licensee pays them royalties on sales, then they need to be able to confirm the licensee's sales activities to make sure that royalty payments are accurate. Another example: If licensees license trademarks as well as technology, the licensor needs to monitor the quality of goods produced by the licensee, since poor quality goods can damage the value of their trademark.

Beyond monitoring licensing agreements, licensors must make personnel available to support licensees in a number of areas. For example, the licensees may need training on use of the technology. They may also require technical support, so that when something goes wrong, they can determine how to resolve the problem by using the expertise of the licensor.

The licensor can charge the licensee for its support efforts. Still, licensors should be aware that in licensing their intellectual assets, they need to be prepared to work actively with licensees. The time and expense needed for proper monitoring of licensing agreements can be substantial.

CHAPTER 9
PERFORMANCE BASED CONTRACTING

As indicated earlier in this chapter, the prevailing wisdom in contracting holds that for the great majority of contracts, contractors should be told *what* they should produce and buyers should avoid the temptation of telling them *how* to do their jobs. In recent years, this outlook has been formally captured in an approach to contracting called *performance based contracting*. With performance based contracting, contractors are told what they should deliver in terms of measurable performance outcomes. For example, in describing requirements for designing a new car, one measurable performance outcome can be stated as follows: "The vehicle should achieve a fuel consumption rate of no less than 30 miles per gallon when traveling at 55 miles an hour." Using this approach, it is up to the contractor to figure out how to design and produce deliverables that meet the goals that satisfy the buyer's requirements.

Performance based contracting has three key components to it. First, *measurable performance standards* need to be established. After this has been done, these standards must be incorporated into a *performance work statement*, which is the performance based contracting equivalent of the traditional SOW. Then a *performance assessment plan* must be articulated. The plan describes how the contractor's performance will be assessed against the performance standards. Each of these components will be described in turn.

ESTABLISHING MEASURABLE PERFORMANCE STANDARDS

Measurable performance standards should be developed systematically. They should emerge from a basic statement of a desired outcome. A useful way to do this is to create a *performance requirements summary* (PRS). An example of a PRS is presented in Figure 9.1. As this exhibit shows, you begin by defining a high level desired outcome. In this case, it is to design and build a fuel efficient car. Once the outcome has been identified, the performance objective(s) associated with the outcome should be articulated. In this case, the performance objective is to design and build a car that meets government fuel efficiency standards. Finally, a measurable outcome standard should be stipulated, indicating the *acceptable quality level* (AQL) that must be achieved in order to meet the performance objective. In this case, the outcome standard and AQL is stated to be development of a car that achieves a fuel efficiency rate of *at least* 30 miles per gallon when the car is operating at a speed of 55 miles per hour. In its totality, the PRS gives you an unambiguous sense of results the contractor needs to achieve in order to meet the requirements.

Outcome	Performance Objective	Outcome Standard and AQL
Fuel efficient car	Design and build a car that meets Department of Transportation requirements for fuel efficiency	Program meets pending government requirements scheduled to take effect on 1 January 20XX, so that the car achieves a fuel efficiency rate of at least 30 miles per gallon when running at a speed of 55 miles per hour

Figure 9.1 Performance Requirements Summary (PRS)

The AQL concept is an interesting and enlightened one. Note that the terminology associated with AQL indicates that you are not striving for a perfect solution. Rather, you identify an *acceptable* performance level – something that is good enough. By doing this you are not encouraging second-rate solutions. In fact, your acceptable performance level might be quite rigorous. What you are doing is to establish a performance floor. If the deliverable does not achieve this AQL, then it is not acceptable. If it exceeds the performance level, then that is good, although not required. Because the AQL is articulated in measurable terms, it becomes relatively simple to determine whether or not it is being met.

Establishing a Performance Work Statement

A performance work statement (PWS) is a modern variant of the SOW. The traditional SOW is a narrative statement describing what work should be carried out to achieve contract requirements. Consequently, it tends to be prescriptive, telling contractors what they should do. Achievement of the SOW is important in contracting, because it defines what constitutes acceptable contract performance. If the SOW is not adhered to, the buyer has the right to reject the deliverable.

Unfortunately, the prescriptive character of SOWs often creates a situation where contractors are being told how to do their jobs. This may unduly constrain them from creating better solutions than are captured in the SOW. If SOWs are foisted on them by buyers, it also provides them with excuses for shoddy performance, because if the contract effort goes awry, they can always say: "The buyer forced us to do things this way, even though as experts we knew that their guidance was misdirected."

As with the case of the traditional SOW, the PWS lies at the heart of the operating portion of a contract. It defines what contractors should direct their attention to. However, rather than telling contractors how to do their jobs, it identifies performance standards the deliverable should achieve. When going through the final review of whether contract requirements were met, attention focuses on the extent to which the deliverable actually does what it was supposed to do. Because the performance standards are defined quantitatively, judgments of performance are reasonably objective.

There are many ways the PWS can be crafted. The simplest is to list all the outcome standards and AQLs identified in the third column of the PRS for the entire contract effort. On a large, complex project, this listing may be quite extensive, running into hundreds of items. On simpler projects, it may incorporate only a handful of items.

ARTICULATING A PERFORMANCE ASSESSMENT PLAN

Adherents of performance based contracting abhor vagueness. They understand that a major source of disputes on contracts is conflicting interpretation of whether a contract's terms and conditions have been met. Too often, the contractor says they have, while the buyer asserts that they have not. Use of measurable performance standards helps reduce vagueness. Vagueness can be further diminished by defining clearly how performance standards will be assessed. Consequently, good performance based contracting practice includes developing a performance assessment plan. The plan lays out clearly the methods by which performance will be assessed.

Clearly, the method employed to assess performance may affect the outcome of the assessment effort. Consider the outcome standard and AQL described in Table 9.1. Exactly how do we plan to determine whether a car achieves a fuel efficiency level of at least thirty miles per gallon when traveling at 55 miles per hour? Will our road test be conducted in an environment where the car encounters heavy traffic that forces it to travel at a speed of 45 miles per hour, followed by open roads where it can travel at 65 miles per hour, yielding an *average* speed of 55 miles per hour? Or will the road test be conducted under strong controls on an automobile test track, where it can run at a steady 55 miles per hour for a distance of hundreds of miles?

The performance assessment plan describes carefully the conditions under which assessment tests will be conducted. In doing so, it reduces the likelihood that either the buyer or contractor questions the reliability of the test results. Without defining how the performance test should be conducted, the contractor can argue that the car it produced meets the standards, and cites the results it achieved when testing a prototype car on an automobile test track. Meanwhile, the buyer can dispute this result, suggesting that they wanted the car's performance tested under real world conditions, where cars routinely accelerate and decelerate while being driven. If test conditions have not been properly specified, both parties can stand by their arguments, resulting in an unpleasant dispute.

Performance Based Contracting in Practice

In practice, performance based contracting must be implemented in a flexible way, reflecting the specific circumstances encountered in a contracting environment. For example, on routine contract efforts, tight and demanding performance standards can be adopted for detailed work efforts, while on first-of-a-kind efforts – which are filled with unknowns – it may be possible to establish standards only at the highest level. Similarly, PWSs for IT projects are likely to look different from those on construction projects, and PWSs for major programs different from those of small work efforts.

While the details may vary in approaches to implementing a performance based contracting effort, the general operating principle remains the same: the contract effort should be defined in terms of measurable outcomes, *not* in terms of steps that contractors should take to carry out their jobs. In order to adhere to this principle, it is helpful to create a PRS, then to articulate a PWS based on the PRS, and then to carefully define how contractor performance will be assessed to see whether it meets acceptable quality levels.

Chapter 10
Conclusion

Today's business environment makes the growth of contracting inevitable. This environment requires organizations to be flexible, to respond quickly to market cues, to be lean, and to be cost effective. Contracting helps organizations address each of these imperatives.

Organizations that contract services can be far more *flexible* than those that try to produce everything themselves. Until recently, companies such as IBM boasted that they were totally self-sufficient in producing their products. Then they saw themselves losing ground to more nimble competitors who were able to piece together goods and services using the outputs of contractors.

Through contracting, organizations are also able to *respond to changing market demand quickly*. In the old days, a consulting company that specialized in software development would address increased demand for telecommunications capabilities by hiring new people and training existing staff, a process that could take a year or longer to yield results. With outsourcing, they can acquire the needed capabilities almost immediately.

Contracting helps organizations to *grow lean*. Not long ago, a company's capabilities were closely tied to its size – bigger was viewed as better, since it implied that the company was able to take advantage of economies of scale, had a greater global reach, and had a greater depth of skills and knowledge. Today, large organizations are viewed as cumbersome behemoths that are at a disadvantage when trying to compete against fleeter, leaner adversaries. Their bureaucracies make them rigid and slow moving. They bring to mind the Spanish Armada in its unsuccessful battles against Francis Drake's small and nimble warships.

Finally, when done right, contracting helps organizations *operate more cost effectively*: They don't need to invest heavily in capital improvements when their product lines change; they don't have large payrolls with their associated, costly fringe benefits; and they can shift the burden of holding inventory onto their contractors.

Warning! None of the benefits described here will be realized unless the contracting efforts are implemented intelligently. As stated earlier in this book, there is nothing automatic about effective contracting. The business press is filled with nightmare stories of poorly formulated or badly implemented contracts that ultimately lead to bankruptcy. Effective contracting requires that key staff develop solid contract and procurement management skills.

On projects, for example, project sponsors, project managers, team leaders, and even technical staff need training on contract and procurement principles – both in the buying and the contractor organizations. Project sponsors need contracting skills in order to make sure that the contracted work effort is achievable within the defined budget and schedule constraints. They also must watch out for provisions (or the absence of provisions) that can create problems. While they need to be expert on the nuts and bolts of contracting, their chief contracting concerns on projects should be strategic.

Project managers working on projects should have excellent contract and procurement skills. If they work for the contractor, they need to know what they can and cannot charge to the project. They also need to know what they can and cannot promise customers who ask them for changes to the deliverable or schedule. If they are employed by the buyer organization, they need to be able to monitor the contractor's performance in order to determine whether it is complying with the contract. They also should be aware of the implications associated with requests they make of the contractor – an off-hand inquiry about a change may unintentionally lead to a change whose costs are charged back to the buyer.

Even team leaders and technical team members need to understand contracting and procurement basics. One frequently encountered problem on projects arises when a technical person in the buyer organization suggests a change in specifications that seems reasonable to their technical counterparts in the contractor organization, who then implement the change. Actions like this can have dramatic consequences. Unchecked changes to specifications can affect the technical integrity of the deliverable. They can contribute to increased costs. Most frighteningly, they can lead the buyer to reject the deliverable, since it does not conform to the specifications described in the contract document.

In most organizations that engage in project-based work efforts, people pick up knowledge about contracting and procurement informally. They gain insights through an *ad hoc* apprenticeship system. When they first begin project work, their project manager might ask them to familiarize themselves with the project effort by reading the statement of work that is contained in the contract. This gives them their first insight into the central role of the contract. Later, they may learn that the buyer refuses to pay for equipment purchased because it does not constitute an "allowable cost" item as covered in the contract. So they now learn another lesson about adhering to the contract – operating out of the realm of the contract's defined boundaries might cost you dearly! Finally, at the close of the contract, they see that the buyer refuses to make final payments until the contractor corrects what it claims to be a defect in the deliverable. Since the contractor disagrees with this claim, negotiations are carried out between buyer and contractor, resulting in an agreement to make small adjustments to the deliverable. The contract is now ready to be closed out.

An apprenticeship approach to learning has great value. Lessons gained through hands-on experience have greater impact and last longer than lessons derived from a book. However, the apprenticeship system described here is haphazard, leaving many knowledge "holes." At some point, project staff really need systematic and formal exposure to contracting and procurement principles. The knowledge gained through formal study will, of course, be strengthened by experience. Thus project staff can experience the best of all worlds: they can develop a deep understanding of contracting and procurement principles through formal study, and achieve practical knowledge through experience.

This book is a first step toward gaining an appreciation of the role of contracting on projects. It has walked the reader through the different stages of the contracting life-cycle and pointed out key issues of importance in each stage. A thorough grasp of the information and insights contained here should help project workers function more effectively in contract environments. However, full mastery of contracting and procurement skills requires taking a second step, a third step … however many steps are needed to achieve mastery of the subject in a given work environment.

INDEX